**VICTORIA'S
STREETCAR
ERA**

His Honour, Lieutenant-Governor
Hugh Nelson steps up onto
car number 1 on the inaugural day
of streetcar service in Victoria,
February 22, 1890.   PABC

VICTORIA'S STREETCAR ERA

Henry Ewert

1992

Sono Nis Press

VICTORIA, B.C., CANADA

Canadian Cataloguing in Publication Data

Ewert, Henry, 1937-
    Victoria's streetcar era

    ISBN 1-55039-023-6

    1. Street-railroads – British Columbia –
Victoria – History. 2. Victoria (B.C.) –
History. I. Title.
TF727.V53E94 1992   388.4'6'0971128   C92-091803-4

This book was published with the assistance of the
Canada Council Block Grant Program.

Published by
SONO NIS PRESS
1745 Blanshard Street
Victoria, B.C., Canada V8W 2J8

Designed and printed in Canada by
MORRISS PRINTING COMPANY LTD.
Victoria, British Columbia

To Dianna
        who loves streetcars
and coffee

Car 5, designated and painted "Beacon Hill Park,"
releases one of its passengers along Niagara Street in 1893.
RONALD A. GREENE COLLECTION

Contents

NATIONAL

ELECTRIC

Tramway and Lighting Co.

(LIMITED LIABILITY.)

———

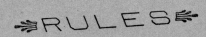 RULES

FOR

CONDUCTORS AND MOTORNEERS.

———

VICTORIA, B. C.:
MUNROE MILLER, PRINTER AND BOOKBINDER.
1892.

Acknowledgements

The idea of creating a book to celebrate the centenary of Victoria's streetcars met with extraordinarily enthusiastic support, not least from Bill Bailey, a transplanted Torontonian who indeed instigated the book, and Patricia Sloan of Sono Nis Press, who gave constant assurance and encouragement from the very beginning.

Jack Porzig's maps, especially drawn for this book, evince the same meticulousness and artistry as his award-winning caboose models and historical essays, and the special drawings by David Reuss demonstrate anew his expertise and generosity.

This book would have been a mere shadow without the surpassing assistance and avid interest of four special contributors: Ronald A. Greene, H. R. "Roly" Halls, Douglas V. Parker, and Robert Turner.

Ted Clark, Geoff Meugens, Bob Webster, and Wallace Young saw to it that I had complete access to their vast Victoria photo collections, and the staffs of both the City of Victoria Archives and the Provincial Archives of British Columbia were tireless in their capacity for assistance, particularly, in the latter case, Brian Young, Brent McBride, and Delphine Castles.

Norris Adams, Frederick F. Angus, George Bergson, Chris Foord, Norman Gidney, Jr., Fred Hall, Mrs. Edith Halls, David Parker, Ernie Les Plant, Allan Prescott, and V. L. Sharman each contributed in significant ways to enrich the book's texture. The countless telephone calls and letters received have made their impact throughout the story, informing, clarifying, and embellishing.

Betty Blair demonstrated beyond all doubt that no one can unscramble a hand-written mélange on foolscap better than she, and type it perfectly to boot.

At Sono Nis Press and Morriss Printing Company, the interest and enthusiasm of Dick Morriss and the artistry and empathy of Jim Bennett made the preparation of this volume a delightful experience. Thanks are also due Peter Corley-Smith for his work with my manuscript in its earlier stages.

Dianna is especially to be praised for prodding and cajoling, for proofreading tirelessly, and for creating optimum working conditions; and to my parents, I am particularly thankful for their love of Victoria, and the consequent romantic images of its streetcars, always with me.

The place itself appears a perfect Eden, in the midst of the dreary wilderness of the North West Coast, and so different is its general aspect, from the wooded, rugged regions around, that one might be pardoned for supposing it had dropped from the clouds into its present position.

JAMES DOUGLAS
Founder of Victoria,
in a letter, 1843

To realize Victoria you must take all that the eye admires most in Bournemouth, Torquay, the Isle of Wight, the Happy Valley at Hong Kong, the Doon, Sorrento, and Camps Bay; add reminiscences of the Thousand Islands, and arrange the whole round the Bay of Naples, with some Himalayas for the background.

RUDYARD KIPLING
Letters to the family, 1907

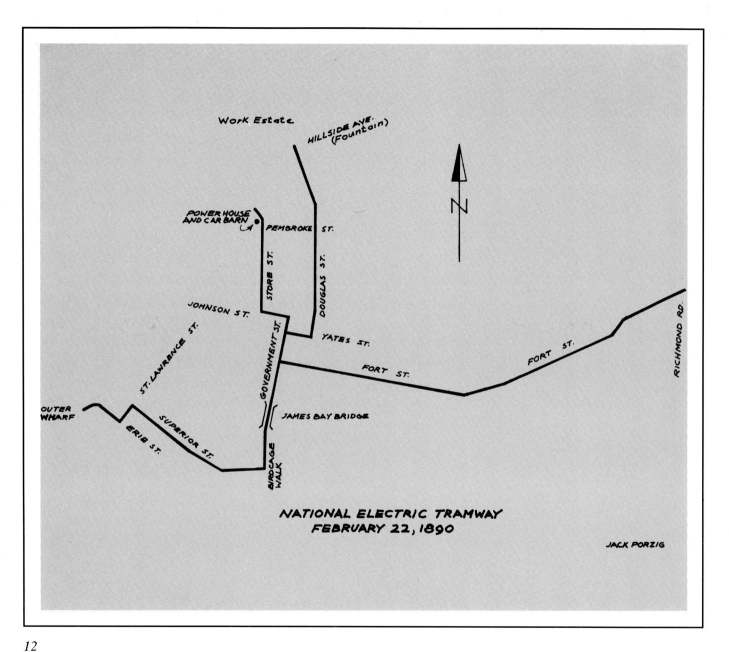

Work Estate

HILLSIDE AVE.
(Fountain)

POWER HOUSE
AND CAR BARN

PEMBROKE ST.

STORE ST.

DOUGLAS ST.

N

JOHNSON ST.

ST. LAWRENCE ST.

GOVERNMENT ST.

YATES ST.

OUTER
WHARF

SUPERIOR ST.

ERIE ST.

JAMES BAY BRIDGE

FORT ST.

FORT ST.

FORT ST.

RICHMOND RD.

BIRDCAGE
WALK

**NATIONAL ELECTRIC TRAMWAY
FEBRUARY 22, 1890**

JACK PORZIG

CHAPTER I

The Victorian Years: *1890-1897*

TO MUCH OF THE WORLD OF 1890, THE CITY OF VICTORIA epitomized isolation. Yet this vibrant community of beautiful gardens and homes on Vancouver Island, off Canada's Pacific coast, actually inaugurated a five-mile streetcar system on February 22 of that year, only the third city in Canada – after Ontario's Windsor and St. Catharines – to offer such sophisticated transport.

Victorians had demanded a railway, and received it when the Esquimalt and Nanaimo Railway was opened on August 13, 1886 with the driving of the last spike by Canada's prime minister, John A. Macdonald. This gave considerable satisfaction as Nanaimo, seventy-two miles north of Victoria, was a mere forty miles across the Strait of Georgia from the C.P.R. in Vancouver. When the E. & N. was extended half a mile east from Esquimalt across a new bridge to its downtown Victoria terminus at Johnson and Store streets on March 29, 1888, the stage was indeed set for British Columbia's largest, and capital, city to launch a streetcar-line building programme.

When David William Higgins, one of Victoria's most notable citizens, and his bride returned home from Seattle on the splendid side-wheeler *Olympian* in April 1889, he "stated to a representative of the Victoria *Standard* newspaper that while in Seattle he had an opportunity of seeing the electric street railway and of testing its much-talked-of merits. It was found to be a complete success [it had begun service on March 19], even surpassing the great cable system in point of comfort and ease of motion. The system adopted by the Seattle Electric railway is the Thomson-Houston, and from one of the promoters it was learned that the road will pay for itself in eighteen months' time."

Victoria's premier newspaper, the *Colonist*, editorialized on May 2, under the heading of "Cheap Fares and Healthy Homes for Victorians," that "in the bylaw before us the city is asked to guarantee interest at the rate of five per centum per annum on a loan of $40,000 for 20 years. No obligation is incurred by the city beyond the payment of the interest should the company fail to earn it. To guard against the possibility of wrong-doing the city is to be represented on the board of directors of the company and periodical audits on behalf of the city are to be made of the company's books. This will be a strong guarantee that the municipality's interests will be conserved and protected so far as the operations of the company are concerned and will prevent even the possibility of the money raised on the faith of the city's guarantee being applied to other than tramway purposes.

"The amount proposed to be guaranteed under the bylaw amounts to only $2,000 per annum, or one-twenty-eighth of one per cent, of the revenue as it stood last year; and it is expressly provided that the special rate shall not increase the total rate of taxation."

When voters took to the polls on May 14 to deal with the tramway bylaw, streetcars were ringingly endorsed, and were a second time as well, on June 11, after the legality of the first vote had been questioned: the May 14 poll had been held between 10 a.m. and 4 p.m. rather than the legal 8 a.m. to 4 p.m. period.[1]

Four days later, the directors of the National Electric Tramway and Lighting Company Limited awarded contracts for constructing the line and installing the electrical plant. T. W. Paterson, of the firm of Bell, Larkin & Paterson, who had built two sections of the E. & N. Railway, secured the track construction, to be of heavy girder rails and ties, completed by November 1. F. H. Osgood, president of the streetcar system in Seattle (seventy miles southeast of Victoria), acquired the contracts for electrical construction, the system to be employed being that of Boston's Thomson-Houston Company.[2] Two days later, the *Colonist* noted that "Four first class 16-foot passenger coaches were ordered by telegraph yesterday from Patterson & Corbin, builders, of St. Catharines. The cars are intended for the electric tramway, and will be the finest tramway cars on the coast. They will have a seating capacity of from 60 to 70." Even the Vancouver *World* took an interest in Victoria's excitement by reporting that "the rails for the Victoria electric tramway have been ordered from Antwerp, and will reach the province in six or eight weeks. The C.P.R. have guaranteed to make up a special train, and rush the rails through from Montreal to Victoria in ten days."

Contractors, Messrs. Lyne and Milne, began construction on September 2 of the power house and car barn, between Constance and Store streets, north of Discovery Street. The Chemainus Mill Company already had the contract for supplying 450 cedar poles to the tramway company for the support of overhead wire; cut near Chemainus, they were brought to Victoria's outer wharf, whence they were teamed into the city by James Baker, who also had the contract to paint and prepare them.

Events had certainly proceeded with dispatch since November 20, 1888, when an agreement had been signed between the city and James Douglas Warren,[3] successful over H. F. Heisterman in bidding to establish a streetcar system and supply electric power, and his colleagues, Andrew Gray, foundry owner; D. W. Higgins, author, former *Colonist* owner, and Speaker to be of the legislature; Joseph Hunter; and Thomas Shotbolt, druggist – Victorians all. On April 6, 1889, the National Electric Tramway and Lighting Company Limited had been incorporated by an act of the legislature of British Columbia, capital authorized at $250,000, and on May 20, six days after the first vote on the tramway bylaw, a large number of the company's shareholders had met for the purpose of electing directors. The *Standard* had reported that "a heavy vote was cast, with the following result: Messrs. T. J. Jones, Jos. Hunter, D. W. Higgins, G. L. Milne, M. H. Cowan, H. F. Heisterman and W. G. Cameron were chosen directors for the ensuing term. Messrs. P. R. Brown and R. Erskine were appointed auditors. The new board met after the adjournment of the shareholders and elected the following officers: President and managing director, D. W. Higgins, M.P.P.; vice-president, G. L. Milne, M.D.; secretary-treasurer, H. F. Heisterman."

Track laying of the two streetcar lines, using mostly thirty-eight-pound girder rail – easier for road traffic to deal with than T-rail – began with the arrival on September 20 at outer wharf of the steamer *City of Pueblo* with fourteen tons of rail.[4] The number one line would operate from outer wharf, via Erie, St. Lawrence, and Superior streets, to Government Street (Birdcage Walk, at its southern end), then east on Yates Street to Douglas Street, and north on Douglas to the Fountain (Hillside Avenue). The number two line would proceed south on Store Street from the car barn (just south of Rock Bay Bridge), east on Johnson Street to Government Street, south on Government to Fort Street, and east on Fort, using fifty-six-pound T-rail as far as Yates Street, past the palatial home

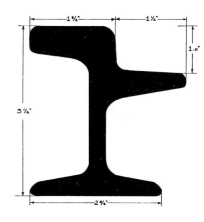

VICTORIA'S ORIGINAL GIRDER RAIL

COLLECTION OF RONALD A. GREENE

DRAWN BY J. PORZIG

16

(at 1501) of D. W. Higgins, Regent's Park, to Jubilee Hospital (then under construction) at Richmond Road, the city limits.

The November 9 edition of the *Colonist* imparts a sense of the excitement generated by the arrival of two of the four streetcars, numbers 1 and 4. (Numbers 2 and 3 would arrive on November 13.)

Two handsome streetcars for the Victoria Electric Railway arrived by the 'Rithet' yesterday morning and drew many a curious visitor to the C. P. N. Cos. wharf during the day. The new cars are well and substantially built, with the bodies sixteen feet long. All the inside work is of ash, with furnishings of cherry and trimmings of solid brass, polished. The seats are of the shaped and perforated pattern, and each car has twelve double side and four end windows. The motor boxes are under the car and between the front and rear trucks. The seating capacity is 30 to a car, while in a pinch 60 passengers can be crowded on board by the 'move up' process. Lighted with electricity and provided with electric bells worked on dry batteries, the cars are complete in all their appointments. One of those already arrived is to run from Work Estate and Douglas Street to the outer wharf; the other is labelled, 'Rock Bay and E & N Ry. Fort Street and Jubilee Hospital.'

By early February 1890 the overhead wire and the ground return wire had been installed (still to be in use for a few years), and on the nineteenth, car number 3 ventured out onto Store Street for a few short sprints, under the direction of Superintendent J. S. Winslow, with conductor J. Sparks along to assist. As the *Colonist* so deftly related, "The gong clanged, the motoneer [*sic*] pulled his lever and the wheels turned. He pulled the lever a little more; the magic power took hold and with a slight whistling noise on the wire above, the car darted forward at a rate of from 8 to 12 miles per hour. [The agreement signed between the city and company provided that the speed of the cars should 'never exceed ten miles an hour.'] Four ladies coming from Esquimalt arrived just in time to get on board and have their first ride in an electrical car in British Columbia."

President Higgins, based in his new office in the power house, had directed and observed the test run with pleasure.

On the day following, the newspaper reported that

The FIRST TRIP to James Bay was taken this morning by a party of gentlemen in one of the electric street railway cars. Mayor Grant, Messrs. Wm. Wilson, Charles Hayward and others were on board. Mr. D. W. Higgins, President of the Company was also on board. The run over the line was very successful, but a few delays were occasioned by frozen dirt on the tracks. The trip over the bridge showed the structure was not affected notably by the weight of the car and to be fully satisfied on the matter, Mayor Grant and Mr. Higgins took a position in the middle of the bridge and had the car driven rapidly past them.

The vibration was not as perceptible as that caused by a heavily-loaded wagon, so the fears of the people that the bridge would suffer from two cars can now be allayed.

Along Superior Street extra speed was put on and the car whizzed along at a great rate, no jar or rocking being noticeable. Mr. Higgins says he hopes everything will be ready for Saturday afternoon when the cars will be put on the run regularly.

Car 3 found itself unable to attain outer wharf, a collapsed culvert at St. Lawrence Street the culprit.

But Saturday, February 22, was the long-awaited day! The *Colonist*'s report was thoroughly in the day's spirit, headed by "Open for Traffic. The Street Service Formally Placed in Operation – An Important Event."

Yesterday witnessed the celebration of two very important events; the one fraught with the greatest importance to the American people, the other marking a new epoch in the progressive history of Victoria. The first, the anniversary of Washington's birth, was quietly observed by all good Americans; the second, the official opening of the street car system, filled all the streets along the line with interested and enthusiastic men, women and children, and was made a day of general civic rejoicing.

Pursuant to invitations issued, about two hundred prominent gentlemen gathered at the power house, Rock Bay bridge, at 1:30 p.m., where they were cordially received by the president of the street railway, Hon. D. W. Higgins, and the other officers of the road, who escorted their guests through the engine and car rooms, etc., and explained the, in some respects, mysterious workings of the system.

Champagne was next opened, and all present drank to the success of the road so auspiciously inaugurated. Then Mr. Edward Allen, M.P.P. for Lillooet, suggested that it would certainly be in order to sing 'God Save the Queen', and the suggestion, with smiles and laughter, carried out with a vim, the member for Lillooet leading the choir.

At about 2 o'clock, cars Nos. 1, 2, 3 and 4, which were waiting on the bridge, were boarded by the company, and all prepared themselves for the excursion over the line. His Honor, the Lieut. Governor [Hugh Nelson], accompanied by his private secretary, Mr. Herbert Stanton, Premier Robson, Mayor Grant and the City Council, members of the Provincial Cabinet and Legislature, the Bench of British Columbia, and many of Victoria's business and professional men composed the party, and when all were seated, His Honor advanced to the front platform of car No. 1 and, bowing to the citizens who thronged the roadway, and sidewalks, he said: Mr. President, ladies and gentlemen. It is with great pleasure that I have accepted the invitation to start this car and formally declare the line open. The completion of this road, in my mind, marks a new era in the progress of Victoria and, judging by the rapid strides with which the city has advanced of late, it is safe to anticipate that the undertaking will be a financially successful one to the promoters. I sincerely hope that our best anticipation will be fully realized.

President Higgins, on behalf of the company, briefly thanked His Honor for his kindly expressed good wishes and assured him that nothing would be left undone by the company to provide the public with a safe and satisfactory service, and the Lieut. Governor then called for three cheers for the new road, which were given with a will. He then turned the motor lever and the wheels of car No. 1 began to revolve fast and faster as it passed down Store street, followed by its three companions at a speed of about ten miles an hour.

The run to the outer wharf was made in eleven minutes, cars were changed, and seventeen minutes later the cars were at the fountain at the junction of Government and Douglas streets, the full speed being shown on the Douglas Street grade. From the Fountain to the Jubilee hospital, the terminus of the Fort Street route, was made in about 20 minutes; and the excursionists then returned to the power house, where they dispersed, after wishing the road long continued prosperity. During the remainder of the day the cars made regular trips being crowded with passengers, and the conductors had their hands full of business. In the evening they were brilliantly illuminated, and filled with passengers, dashed through the streets in busy, metropolitan style; the admiration of all lovers of enterprise, convenience and progress.

Wheeling from Beacon Hill Park, car 6 rounds onto Douglas Street from Yates Street, soon to pass City Hall, on the left, and St. John's "Iron" Church in the distance, the site of Hudson's Bay department store today.
AUTHOR'S COLLECTION

President and managing director of the National Electric Tramway and Lighting Company Limited, David William Higgins. PABC

Car 16 makes contact with Fort Street's sidewalk after failing to make the left turn onto Fort Street from Oak Bay Avenue. This one-of-a-kind vehicle had worse in store for it.
RONALD A. GREENE COLLECTION

Part of the National Electric Tramway's fleet – number 5 at far right – shows off on Rock Bay Bridge, just north of the car barn. PABC

Car 14 pauses with a picturesque sextet at Fort Street and Oak Bay Avenue prior to its return downtown. PABC

Two B.C. Electric streetcars, car 11 on the right, scurry eastward on Niagara Street, having just crossed Government Street. The lacrosse match at Caledonia Park seems even to have temporarily stopped bread deliveries.

VICTORIA CITY ARCHIVES

The terminus of the Esquimalt line,
Grafton Street, with Saint Paul's
Anglican Church, in two views.
The photo above with car 6
was taken before the Point Ellice disaster,
the one below after the tragedy,
when all the bridges and trestles crossed
by the street railway were evaluated.
Within a few years, the railway was laid
on the left side, but not on the trestle.
PABC

Government Street on James Bay Bridge, south from the present site of the Empress Hotel to the old parliament buildings.   RONALD A. GREENE COLLECTION

Seven streetcars,
led by double-trucked
number 13, line up
at Oak Bay Park,
today's Windsor Park,
to take home the crowds
from a lacrosse game.
PABC

Car 16 and Point Ellice Bridge
combined to take 55 people
to their deaths on May 26, 1896.
AUTHOR'S COLLECTION

A Beacon Hill Park–Spring Ridge car swings from Yates Street south onto Government Street.   PABC

Goldstream powerhouse, the first hydro-electric development on Vancouver Island. VICTORIA CITY ARCHIVES

Regular service began on Sunday at 9 a.m., with a fare of five cents, and within two weeks there was much talk about a new line to Beacon Hill.

On April 7, a gang of surveyors began laying out a new 3.2-mile streetcar line which would cross Rock Bay Bridge from the end of track at the north end of Store Street, and venture west over Point Ellice Bridge along Esquimalt Road to Esquimalt. By September 13, the laying of the fifty-six-pound T-rail was completed (most of it was at the side of the road), and on October 9, a trial run over the length of the line was made in preparation for its inaugural day, Sunday, October 12.[5]

Meanwhile, two more streetcars, 5 and 6, had arrived, and on the twenty-third of October, cars 7, 8 and 9 would be placed in service – painted green – on the Esquimalt line.

On the following day, Esquimalt cars began operating from the north end of Rock Bay Bridge to Esquimalt, rather than from Government and Yates streets, to allow for the strengthening of the bridge; the regular pattern resumed on November 14.

On the twenty-third of October, the Douglas-Outer Wharf line had instituted a twenty-minute service between 6 a.m. and 11:35 p.m.

For the National Electric Tramway, somewhat more than ten months of streetcar operation in 1890 had produced encouraging receipts of $38,705.

As 1891 got underway, the capacity of the power house was being increased, and on April 9, tenders were called for a fourth streetcar line, 7,897 feet in length, from Oak Bay beach, west on Oak Bay Avenue, connecting with the Jubilee Hospital run at Fort Street. (Coincidentally, the Oak Bay Land & Improvement Company had been created with the intention of attracting "a good class of residents.") The Oak Bay shuttle service began operating at 6 a.m. on July 1.[6] Fortunately, two more streetcars, 10 and 11, employed at first as motorless trailers, had been placed in service on April 29.

The fifth line – actually a 3,900-foot extension east from Jubilee Hospital to Driving Park – was opened for service on September 26, merely a month since surveys for it had begun![7] (Driving Park would be developed over the years into the Willows, the Victoria area's exhibition park.) Both of these new streetcar lines had been laid with forty-pound, conventional T-rail, acceptable in areas of very little road traffic.

A sixth line, well over a mile in length, opened on December 23, when Spring Ridge, a major source of drinking water for so many years, was connected with Douglas Street, via Gladstone and Chambers streets, Caledonia Avenue, Cook Street, and Pandora Avenue.[8] This new route, to become known as the Pandora, and later, the Fernwood line, was to have been ready earlier, but out of deference to public opinion, the thirty-eight-pound rail (identical to the original rail through most of the system) laid on Pandora Avenue at the side of the road was re-laid in the middle of the street.

Four new cars, 12 to 15, had been placed in service late in the year, 12 and 13 being the company's first double-trucked streetcars. Receipts for the year, $78,000, and a loan of $100,000 had allowed the company to show a net profit of $18,000.

An unusual streetcar, number 16, arrived in Victoria on February 18, 1892; the company must have struck a special deal with the Newburyport Car Manufacturing Company, just north of Boston, for this one car was identical to a series of forty-five delivered for use in Boston between December 1891 and March 1892. This relatively large streetcar operated on three axles (six wheels) rather than on one or two trucks, with the centre axle known as a Robinson radial truck, patented. This peculiar streetcar would yet leave its mark on Victoria, and transportation, history.

A seventh line, a three-quarter-mile northward extension of the Douglas Street line, to Tolmie Avenue, went into service on March 12 as a shuttle operation, but only for two days, after which it was integrated into the Douglas-Outer Wharf run.[9]

Yet another line, just under three-quarters of a mile in length, the Beacon Hill extension, began operating on June 30, virtually unannounced and with only a few runs.[10] The following day saw full operation on this line – now connected with the Pandora line – which branched off the Outer Wharf run at Menzies Street and proceeded south before bending east on Niagara Street to terminate at Douglas Street, across the road from Beacon Hill Park. Both of these extensions had been laid with the usual girder rail.

Regular service on the Esquimalt line had been interrupted twice during June and July by concerns about the bridge at Point Ellice. Apparently, the activities of teredo worms, as well as the deterioration through rot of the wooden timbers, caused the bridge actually to sink a few feet. Indeed, the bridge at Rock Bay and the smaller culverts and trestling along the line to Esquimalt made it a constant source of worry for the company.

Tragedy struck, not at Point Ellice Bridge, but at Store Street on the morning of August 7 when a quickly out-of-control fire destroyed the power house. It seems almost a miracle that the adjacent car barn, with its streetcars, survived.[11] Work began immediately on a new $16,300 power house – still there today – closer yet to Rock Bay Bridge. Meanwhile the Westminster and Vancouver Tramway lent the company two Edison generators, allowing limited streetcar service to resume on September 24. That the power house blaze hampered not only business, but also pleasure, was graphically demonstrated when the Jockey Club, whose horse racing meet at Driving Park would be negatively affected by the lack of streetcar service, operated the trailers, cars 10 and 11, from September 8 to 10, drawn by horses from Fort and Government streets.[12]

When on May 24, 1893 one span of the Point Ellice Bridge sank four feet while a streetcar was making a crossing,[13] new company manager, F. N. McCready was forcibly reminded of the streetcar system's vulnerability. (Higgins, almost frantically busy after the fire, and at the same time Speaker of British Columbia's Legislative Assembly, had tendered his resignation on January 11.)

The opening of the Mount Baker Hotel at the beach at Oak Bay on June 8 was a delightful event,[14] but the crash of the New York stock market on June 27 precipitated a world-wide depression which exacerbated the financial squeeze the company was already experiencing, brought on by its limited capitalization and by expenditures necessary to cope with unforeseen difficulties, such as the heavy snows of February which had shut down the system for almost a week, but chiefly the power house fire and its aftermath. Would the city perhaps buy out the company? An offer too good to refuse appeared from London, England: Messrs. Sperling and Company was ready to grant the company £100,000, and the company's directors accepted Sperling's terms. Because the word "tramway" was unacceptable to the English company, and since the Victoria company for assistance had indeed consented to Sperling's terms, a special act of the provincial legislature created a new entity on April 6, 1894: Victoria Electric Railway and Lighting Company Limited, in place of National Electric Tramway.

The new winter schedule of January 4, 1894 had shown Esquimalt streetcars again operating from the power house, at the south end of Rock Bay Bridge, taking thirty-five minutes for the journey to Esquimalt, and charging ten cents – five cents for shorter journeys to and from various points on the line. The double-trucked cars, 12 and 13, provided service for the Esquimalt line, while cars 1, 2, 3, 4, 7 and 8 serviced Douglas–Outer Wharf; cars 5 and 6, Pandora–Beacon Hill; cars 9 and 16, Fort Street; and car 15, the Oak Bay shuttle. (Cars 10 and 11 were still non-motored, and 14 was unaccounted for, in terms of route assignment).

The motorneers were receiving some much-needed respite in the company's programme of enclosing, and to a degree weather-proofing, the vestibules at both ends of the cars. Another welcome refinement in 1894 was the beginning of the designation of stops for the streetcars, gradually removing the system from the haphazard, increasingly dangerous fashion of stopping wherever passengers beckoned. Late in the year, the company acquired three more streetcars, orphaned by the demise of the street railway line in Port Townsend, Washington; they were numberered 17, 18 and 19.

Victoria acquired a second steam railroad with the beginning of service on June 2 of the Victoria and Sidney Railway, a seventeen-mile route connecting Sidney to Victoria. The Victoria depot, though temporary, was easily accessible to streetcar patrons, merely a block east of Douglas Street on Tolmie Avenue, the northern terminus of the streetcar line.[15]

By year's end, the V.E.R. & L. Co. found itself in a more precarious predicament than a year ago, now over $30,000 more in debt and searching for a purchaser. With the advent of 1895, more money, $109,055, soon arrived from Sperling and Company, but by the end of May, the company was $84,375 in debt.

By the end of April, the company had established eleven-acre Oak Bay recreation park (today's Windsor Park) at the end of the

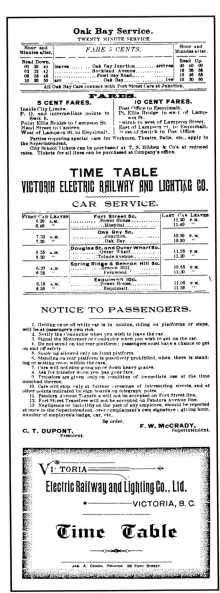

<table>
<tr><th colspan="3">Douglas St. & Outer Wharf & Connections
TEN MINUTE SERVICE.</th></tr>
</table>

Hour and Minutes after.	FARE 5 CENTS	Hour and Minutes after.
Read Down.		Read Up.
50 00 15 20 30 40	lvs......Tolmie Avenue.....arr.	40 50 00 10 20 30
55 05 15 25 35 45	.............Fountain.............	35 45 55 05 15 25
00 10 20 30 40 50	.............City Hall.............	30 40 50 00 10 20
05 15 25 35 45 55	...........Broughton St...........	25 35 45 55 05 15
10 20 30 40 50 00	...........Menzies St.............	20 30 40 50 00 10
15 25 35 45 55 05	arr........Outer Wharf.......lvs.	15 25 35 45 55 05

Cars leaving Fountain and Outer Wharf at 15, 35 and 55 minutes after the hour, connect with Fort Street going up.

Cars leaving Fountain and Outer Wharf at 05, 25 and 45 minutes after the hour, connect with Fort Street going down.

Cars leaving Fountain and Outer Wharf at 15 minutes after the hour connect with Esquimalt half hour car at Campbell's Corner.

Cars leaving Fountain and Outer Wharf at 25 and 45 minutes after the hour connect with Fort Street cars going down, and with Esquimalt cars at Power House.

Cars leaving Fountain at 05 and 35 minutes after the hour, and Outer Wharf at 25 and 55 minutes after connect with Pandora Avenue going up.

Cars leaving Fountain at 25 and 55 and Outer Wharf at 05 and 35 minutes after the hour connect with Beacon Hill car going up.

Spring Ridge and Beacon Hill.
THIRTY MINUTE SERVICE.

Hour and Minutes after.	FARE 5 CENTS.	Hour and Minutes after.
Read Down.		Read Up.
20 50	leaves............Fernwood............arrives	20 50
27 57	.............Cook Street.............	13 43
30 00	.............City Hall.............	10 40
35 05	...........Broughton St...........	05 35
40 10	...........Menzies Street...........	00 30
45 15	arr..........Beacon Hill.........lvs	55 25

All above cars make close connections with Douglas Street cars at City Hall, and with Outer Wharf cars at Menzies Street.

Cars leaving Fernwood 20 minutes after, and Beacon Hill at 25 minutes after the hour, make close connections with Fort Street going down, and with Esquimalt cars at Power House.

Cars leaving Fernwood at 50 minutes after the hour, and Beacon Hill at 05 minutes after the hour, make close connections with Fort Street going up.

Cars leaving Fernwood at 20 minutes after and Beacon Hill at 55 minutes after the hour, make close connection with Esquimalt half hour car at Campbell's Corner.

Fort Street and Jubilee Hospital.

Hour and Minutes after.	FARE 5 CENTS.	Hour and Minutes after.
Read Down.		Read Up.
00 30 40	leaves.........Power House.........arrives	40 00 20
05 25 45	...Cor. Fort and Government Sts...	35 55 15
10 30 50	.........Vancouver Street.........	30 50 10
14 34 54	...........Moss Street...........	26 46 06
17 37 57	.........Oak Bay Junction.........	23 43 03
20 40 00	arr......Jubilee Hospital.....lvs	20 40 00

Cars leaving Hospital at 20 and 40 minutes after the hour connect with Esquimalt car at Power House.

All cars leaving the Power House and Hospital connect with cars going up Douglas Street, and cars going to Outer Wharf.

Cars leaving Hospital at 20 minutes after the hour, connect with Beacon Hill or Pandora Avenue.

Cars leaving Power House on the hour connect with Pandora Avenue and Beacon Hill at Fort Street, corner Government.

Esquimalt Service.

Hour and Minutes after.	FARE.—St. George's Switch, 5 cents. Esquimalt 10 cents.	Hour and Minutes after.
Read Down.		Read Up.
— 38	leaves.........Campbell's Corner.........arrives	— 30
05 40	.............Power House.............	05 25
10 45	...........Craigflower Road...........	55 20
15 50	...........St. George's Switch...........	50 15
17 52	.............Head Street.............	48 13
19 54	...........Lampson Street...........	46 11
22 57	...........Admirals Road...........	43 08
25 00	.............Canteen.............	40 05
27 02	arr...........Esquimalt.........lvs	37 02

Cars leaving Esquimalt at 37 minutes after the hour, making close connection at Power House with Fort Street going up, and connect with Douglas St. or Outer Wharf cars at Fort Street, corner Government.

Cars leaving Esquimalt at 02 minutes after the hour connect at Campbell's Corner with Beacon Hill and Outer Wharf cars, or wait 5 minutes for connections with Pandora Avenue or Douglas Street cars.

Oak Bay streetcar line. Although the major aim of the company had been to motivate ridership, it did enhance an already attractive community with a 2,000-seat grandstand, a bicycle track, and a field for Canada's national sport, lacrosse.[16]

But when in late May Dunsmuir and Sons and the Union Colliery Company served the company with a writ for their account for the power plant's coal usage, and the Bank of Montreal followed on June 1 with another writ, the Victoria Electric Railway and Lighting Company Limited went into receivership, with John McKilligan, the company's secretary, and Henry Croft appointed interim receivers on June 4.

McKilligan worked with diligence, even travelling to London, to encourage Sperling and Company to take over the Victoria company, and his intense efforts paid off as Sperling and Company took possession of the company on January 8, 1896, appointed McKilligan sole receiver and manager, and then put the company up for sale at the end of the month.

On April 11, Victoria businessman and member of parliament, Frank Stillman Barnard, son of the founder of Barnard's Express (inextricably linked with the Cariboo Road), bid $340,000, beating out bids of $325,000 by Hedley Chapman and $300,000 by C. A. Holland of the B.C. Investment Agency, to purchase the Victoria company for his Consolidated Railway and Lighting Company, which had been formed, to the day, two years earlier with an authorized capital of $1,000,000. At that time, he had purchsed the floundering Vancouver street railway system for $290,000 and, on April 13, 1895, the similarly distressed Westminster and Vancouver Tramway for $280,000. When Barnard took possession of the Victoria company on May 1, 1896, he owned all three British

31

Columbia systems, and the fate of the Victoria company was forever out of the hands of Victorians.

The two major creditors of the Vancouver and New Westminster systems, the Bank of British Columbia and the Yorkshire Corporation, had actually formed the Consolidated Railway and Lighting Company, which thereupon kept a watchful eye on the Victoria system. Indeed, Barnard, in 1895, had arranged with a representative of Sperling and Company, R. M. Horne-Payne, to advance funds to the Consolidated company.

On April 17, 1896, by special act of the provincial legislature, the Consolidated company increased its capitalization to $1,500,000 and simplified its title to Consolidated Railway Company.

Within a month, a new open-sided streetcar arrived, number 20, a car which would function in a few years as a sightseeing vehicle, but would finish its working life with its sides enclosed.

The Victoria system at this time consisted of 12.8 miles (67,589 feet) of streetcar line, all single-tracked, with an additonal 2,529 feet of thirty-eight-pound girder rail comprising two turnouts and ten sidings: turnouts were located at the Oak Bay terminal and at Jubilee Hospital, and sidings were in place on Fort Street at Vancouver Street, at the school (Fernwood Road) and at Belmont Street; on Oak Bay Avenue at Foul Bay Road; on Douglas Street at Hillside Avenue and in front of the city hall; on Store Street at Pembroke Street; on Superior Street; on Caledonia Avenue; and on Esquimalt Road.

During May the company's new local manager of the physical plant, A. T. Goward, had taken a thorough-going inventory of the Victoria system, assessing the value of all its assets. His streetcar valuations amounted to $56,720.65.

CONSOLIDATED RAILWAY CO'Y,
(VICTORIA BRANCH.)

Summer Time Table, 1896,
FROM MAY 1ST.

	WEEK DAY SERVICE.		SUNDAY SERVICE.	
	FIRST CAR LEAVES A.M.	LAST CAR LEAVES P.M.	FIRST CAR LEAVES A.M.	LAST CAR LEAVES P.M.
1. Fort Street Service.				
Power House to Jubilee Hospital	6.00	11.00	9.40	10.20
Jubilee Hospital to Power House	6.20	11.20	10.00	10.40
TWENTY MINUTE SERVICE from Power House from 6.00 a.m. until noon, and from 8 p.m. until 11 p.m.				
TEN MINUTE SERVICE from corner Government and Yates Streets to Jubilee Hospital, from 12.05 p.m. until 7.55 p.m. Sundays until 6 p.m.				
2. Oak Bay Service.				
Oak Bay Junction to Oak Bay	6.20	10.30	9.50	9.40
Oak Bay to Oak Bay Junction	6.30	10.50	10.10	9.50
TWENTY MINUTE SERVICE from 6.20 a.m. until 10.30 p.m. Sundays until 9.50 a.m.				
3. Douglas Street and Outer Wharf Service.				
Outer Wharf to Tolmie Avenue	6.15	10.55	9.55	10.15
Tolmie Avenue to Outer Wharf	6.30	10.50	9.50	10.10
TWENTY MINUTE SERVICE from 6.15 a.m. until 10.55 p.m.				
4. Spring Ridge and Beacon Hill Service.				
Beacon Hill to Spring Ridge	6.25	10.55	9.55	10.15
Spring Ridge to Beacon Hill	6.20	10.50	9.50	10.20
HALF HOUR SERVICE from 6.20 a.m. until 10.55 p.m.				
5. Esquimalt Service.				
Power House to Esquimalt	6.05	11.05	9.40	11.05
Campbell's Corner to Esquimalt	6.35	10.35	10.35	10.35
Esquimalt to Power House	6.35	11.25	10.00	11.25
HALF HOUR SERVICE from 6.05 a.m. until noon, and from 8 p.m. until 11 p.m. from Power House to Esquimalt.				
TWENTY MINUTE SERVICE from 12.15 p.m. until 7.55 p.m. from Campbell's Corner to Esquimalt. Sundays until 6 p.m.				

Special Cars may be engaged on application.
This Time Table may be changed at any time without notice.

F. S. BARNARD,
President Consolidated Railway Co.

JOHN B. McKILLIGAN,
Manager Victoria Branch Con. R'y Co.

Victoria, 1st May, 1896.

CONSOLIDATED RAILWAY CO'Y

(VICTORIA BRANCH.)

Winter Time Table, 1896-7

FROM 10th NOVEMBER, 1896.

	WEEK DAY SERVICE.		SUNDAY SERVICE.	
	FIRST CAR LEAVES A.M.	LAST CAR LEAVES P.M.	FIRST CAR LEAVES A.M.	LAST CAR LEAVES P.M.
1. FORT STREET SERVICE.				
Post Office to Jubilee Hospital	6.30	11.00	9.15	10.15
Jubilee Hospital to Post Office	6.45	11.15	9.30	10.30
FIFTEEN MINUTE SERVICE from 6.30 a. m. until 11.00 p. m.				
2. OAK BAY SERVICE.				
Oak Bay Junction to Oak Bay	6.45	10.15	9.20	9.15
Oak Bay to Oak Bay Junction	7.00	10.30	9.30	9.30
HALF HOUR SERVICE from 6.45 a. m. until 10.15 p. m.				
3. DOUGLAS STREET SERVICE.				
Post Office to Tolmie Avenue	6.30	10.30	9.30	10.00
Tolmie Avenue to Post Office	6.45	10.45	9.15	10.15
HALF HOUR SERVICE from 6.30 a. m. until 10.30 p. m.				
4. OUTER WHARF SERVICE.				
Post Office to Outer Wharf	6.30	10.30	9.30	10.00
Outer Wharf to Post Office	6.45	10.40	9.15	10.10
HALF HOUR SERVICE from 6.30 a. m. until 10.30 p. m.				
5. SPRING RIDGE SERVICE.				
Post Office to Spring Ridge	6.45	10.15	9.15	10.15
Spring Ridge to Post Office	7.00	10.30	9.30	10.30
HALF HOUR SERVICE from 6.45 a. m. until 10.15 p. m.				
6. BEACON HILL SERVICE.				
Post Office to Beacon Hill	6.45	10.15	9.15	10.15
Beacon Hill to Post Office	7.00	10.30	9.30	10.30
HALF HOUR SERVICE from 6.45 a. m. until 10.15 p. m.				
7. ESQUIMALT SERVICE.				
Post Office to Esquimalt	6.30	10.30	9.30	10.00
Esquimalt to Post Office	7.05		9.35	
Esquimalt to Power House		11.00		10.30
HALF HOUR SERVICE from 6.30 a. m. until 10.30 p. m.				

☞ SPECIAL CARS MAY BE ENGAGED ON APPLICATION ☜

☞ THIS TIME TABLE MAY BE CHANGED AT ANY TIME WITHOUT NOTICE ☜

For Receiver, Consolidated Railway Company,

JOHN B. McKILLIGAN,

Victoria, 10th November, 1896.   Manager Victoria Branch.

COLONIST PRESSES

But on the sunniest, most carefree of celebration days, the world of Victoria and its pretty little streetcar system came crashing to death and darkest confusion. At 1:50 p.m. on Tuesday, May 26, the final of three days of celebration of Queen Victoria's birthday, three-axled car 16, with 142 passengers, had just begun its westward crossing of eleven-year-old Point Ellice Bridge. Its destination, as that of car 6 ahead of it, just leaving the bridge, was Esquimalt and the intricate military manoeuvres the militia from the Victoria barracks and the naval forces based at Esquimalt would perform on the parade ground there. It was to be a gala time.

Harry Talbot, the conductor who had been on the streetcar two years earlier when Point Ellice Bridge had shaken frighteningly, and motorneer George Farr, had come aboard a few minutes earlier at the power house as car 16's new crew. Farr was said to have remarked upon realizing the extent of the crowding in car 16 and on its open vestibules that "if we get over the bridge, we'll be lucky,"[17] and chances are he was not talking about delicate Rock Bay Bridge.

Point Ellice Bridge had rocked dangerously when car 6 had made its passage, but when Harry Talbot's car was about thirty-five feet onto the bridge, a resounding snapping sound was heard, the roadway dropping about a foot and a half, but the streetcar proceeded approximately fifteen feet farther. Since the track was on the north side of the bridge, when the span snapped, the streetcar plummeted into the water on its right side, the span with it, in full view of horrified onlookers on the shores. Divers working until nightfall were able to recover forty-eight bodies, and the following day yielded another seven; among the fifty-five dead were George Farr, as well as Harry Talbot who left a widow and four children.

A lengthy official enquiry established that the cause of the disaster was rotted timbers in the floor structure of the bridge. The

City of Victoria, because of its gross negligence in failing to maintain and repair the bridge, was forced to pay more than $150,000 in claims.

Although the Consolidated company was absolved of any responsibility in the disaster, gross overloading of streetcars was an issue that government would deal with in years to come. The company apparently had not been aware of the fact that Point Ellice Bridge was to receive no vehicles of more than ten tons; car 16 had borne a twenty-one-ton load, in this, the worst streetcar accident in North-American history.

Although a temporary ferry service was quickly in service and the Esquimalt and Nanaimo Railway had decked its bridge at Johnson Street to allow pedestrian traffic across, it was not until December 4 that streetcar service resumed across a temporary eighteen-foot-wide bridge immediately south of the fatal bridge.[18]

In the meantime, two small trestles, one very near the Esquimalt terminus, in execrable condition on the Esquimalt line had been removed, and both Rock Bay and James Bay bridges had been closed for repairs. Regarding James Bay Bridge, the company had assured the City of Victoria on June 17 that only eighteen-foot cars, weighing less than 6½ tons (without passengers), carrying a maximum of thirty passengers would operate over the bridge, at least two hundred feet apart. The thirty-passenger rule would be in effect as well on Rock Bay Bridge and the temporary Point Ellice crossing.

If the Consolidated company's situation before the Point Ellice disaster had been somewhat tenuous, especially given the continued depressed state of the economy, it was now, after Point Ellice, extremely delicate. In August, the London-based Railway Amalgamation Syndicate, which had been formed in 1895 by Horne-

Payne and his associates to guarantee funds to the Consolidated company, refused any more aid.

Thus, in financial ruin, the Consolidated Railway Company fell to receiver William Farrell of the Yorkshire Corporation on October 13. No interest was expressed when the Consolidated company was offered for sale on November 17 at public auction in Vancouver, but two weeks later, the company was indeed sold, to the Colonial Railway and Investment Company of eastern Canada.

For £462,000 the Colonial group sold the Consolidated company to a London-based group, incorporated on April 3, 1897 as the British Columbia Electric Railway Company Limited. Fresh capital had been raised by Horne-Payne, a true believer in the future of British Columbia.

The directors of this company were Robert M. Horne-Payne, chairman; Frank S. Barnard, appropriately managing director in British Columbia; J. Horne-Payne; A. C. Mitchell-Innes; R. N. Laurie; G. P. Norton; and R. K. Sperling. Copenhagen-born Vancouver resident Johannes Buntzen was appointed comptroller and general manager, while Rochfort Henry Sperling (of the same family as R. K.) received the post of general superintendent. The Canadian office of B.C. Electric would be in Vancouver.

The misery and murk of the depression would begin to lift within a year's time, unfortunately too late for the local British Columbia visionaries, entrepreneurs, and shareholders of the street railway and interurban systems of Victoria, Vancouver, and New Westminster. Nonetheless, when the transfer of the Consolidated company to the B.C. Electric Company occurred on April 15, inhabitants of the three cities and their environs knew that their precious transportation systems had entered a new, more secure phase of their brief history.

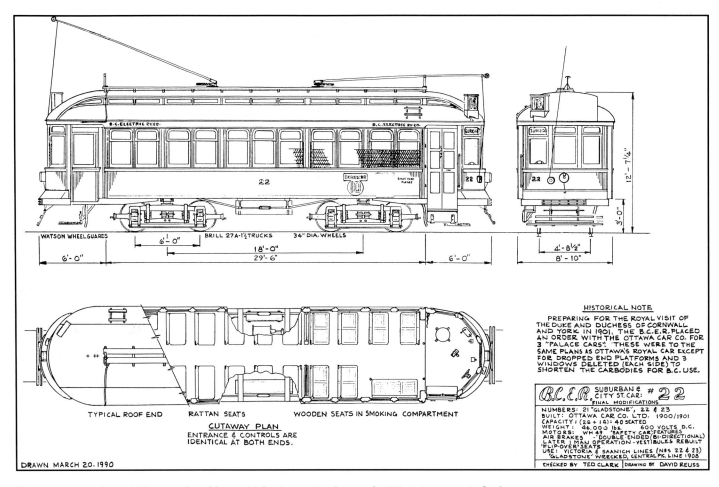

WATSON WHEELGUARDS   BRILL 27A-1½ TRUCKS   34" DIA. WHEELS

6'-0"   6'-0"   18'-0"   6'-0"   6'-0"
29'-6"

4'-8½"
8'-10"

12'-7¼"
3'-0"

TYPICAL ROOF END   RATTAN SEATS   WOODEN SEATS IN SMOKING COMPARTMENT

CUTAWAY PLAN
ENTRANCE & CONTROLS ARE
IDENTICAL AT BOTH ENDS.

DRAWN MARCH 20, 1990

HISTORICAL NOTE
PREPARING FOR THE ROYAL VISIT OF
THE DUKE AND DUCHESS OF CORNWALL
AND YORK IN 1901, THE B.C.E.R. PLACED
AN ORDER WITH THE OTTAWA CAR CO. FOR
3 "PALACE CARS". THESE WERE TO THE
SAME PLANS AS OTTAWA'S ROYAL CAR EXCEPT
FOR DROPPED END PLATFORMS AND 3
WINDOWS DELETED (EACH SIDE) TO
SHORTEN THE CARBODIES FOR B.C. USE.

B.C.E.R. SUBURBAN & # **22**
CITY ST. CAR:
FINAL MODIFICATIONS
NUMBERS: 21 "GLADSTONE", 22 & 23
BUILT: OTTAWA CAR CO. LTD. 1900/1901
CAPACITY: (26 + 14): 40 SEATED
WEIGHT: 46,000 lbs. 600 VOLTS D.C.
MOTORS: WH 49 "SAFETY CAR" FEATURES
AIR BRAKES - DOUBLE-ENDED (BI-DIRECTIONAL)
LATER 1 MAN OPERATION - VESTIBULES REBUILT
"FLIP-OVER" SEATS
USE: VICTORIA & SAANICH LINES (Nos 22 & 23)
"GLADSTONE" WRECKED, CENTRAL PK. LINE 1908
CHECKED BY TED CLARK | DRAWING BY DAVID REUSS

Twin streetcars 22 and 23 were the oldest vehicles in service during the Victoria system's final years.
Both had operated the last year and a half of service on the Saanich interurban line.

CHAPTER II

B.C. Electric's Half Century:
The First Four Decades –
Growth and Dreams, Struggle and Decline

THE *COLONIST* EDITORIALIZED THAT "THE PROVINCE IS RICH–
even beyond our dreams, but we are not. We want people to develop
the wealth we possess. We want to be known by Britain and America."[19] The new British Columbia Electric Railway epitomized the
style of richly-moneyed investment which virtually all British Columbians in 1897 felt was necessary for the province's future.

Although he remained a director of B.C. Electric, Frank S.
Barnard resigned from his post as managing director on April 13,
1898, to be replaced on the following day by Johannes Buntzen. On
April 25, streetcar service was shut down on the final five blocks at
the northern end of Douglas Street (Burnside to Tolmie) because of
the Victoria & Sidney Railway's move to a new depot one block east
of Douglas Street between Market Street and Hillside Avenue.
During 1898 the company inaugurated a 3,500-hp. hydro-electric
plant at Goldstream, fifteen miles west of Victoria, nine years after
the N.E.T. had purchased the property with this development in
mind.

The summer of 1899 saw the completion of a grandiose exhibition building at the Willows fairground,[20] and in November, the

introduction of hand-held, metal fareboxes, to the relief of harassed streetcar conductors.

It was 1901 when Thomas Plimley, owner of a bicycle shop at 1010 Yates Street, brought the first automobile to the Victoria area, a single-cylinder, four-horsepower 1900 Oldsmobile. Costing $6,000 each, three beautiful new streetcars, double-trucked and larger than any other vehicle on the system, arrived in Victoria on March 18; these three Ottawa Car Company products, 21, 22 and 23, were the first of many streetcars to be shipped from Vancouver by barge, then brought south from the new Ladysmith barge slip (replacing the temporary slip at Nanaimo) on E. & N. flatcars.[21] (Car 21 would be returned to Vancouver a week after entering service on May 3 to function as interurban car "Gladstone" on the Vancouver-New Westminster interurban line until its destruction in a tragic collision in November 1908.)

During the summer of 1901, crews completely relaid the track from Oak Bay junction to the Willows. This virtually new branch re-opened, together with Willows Park, on September 12. For the visit of the future King George V to British Columbia from September 30 to October 3, architect Francis Rattenbury outlined the three-year-old parliament buildings' structure and periphery with hundreds of electric lights,[22] an effect so striking that to this day the lights twinkle every day with the onset of dusk.

In 1902, a new car barn on Pembroke Street, facing north, with its western flank along Store Street, was constructed; this handsome, $19,000 brick structure, designed by Rattenbury, housed forty streetcars on eight tracks. In January 1903, the Victoria & Sidney Railway, taken over by the Great Northern in the previous year, opened a new Victoria depot on Cormorant Street, just west of Douglas Street,[23] whose streetcar line it crossed at Fisgard Street. In

TOURISTS AND VISITORS

GUIDE

- TO -

Victoria

TAKE THE STREET CARS

- AND -

Ask Conductors for Information

AS TO REACHING

VARIOUS POINTS OF INTEREST

OFFICERS OF THE COMPANY.

BOARD:

R. M. HORNE PAYNE, ESQ., CHAIRMAN,
R. NORTHALL LAURIE, ESQ.,   ·   ·   ·
A. C. MITCHELL-INNES, ESQ.,   ·   ·   Directors,
J. HORNE PAYNE, ESQ., Q. C.,   ·   ·   London, England.
R. K. SPERLING, ESQ.,   ·   ·   ·   ·
G. P. NORTON, ESQ., ·   ·   ·   ·   ·

F. S. BARNARD, ESQ.,   ·   ·   British Columbia Director.

HEAD OFFICE:

1 & 2 Great Winchester Street, London, England.

J. BUNTZEN, GENERAL MANAGER AND COMPTROLLER,
VANCOUVER, B. C.

J. M. CAMPBELL, ASST. MANAGER AND CHIEF ENGINEER.

A. T. GOWARD, ASST. COMPTROLLER, VICTORIA, B. C.

H. GIBSON, SUPT. OF TRAFFIC, VICTORIA, B. C.

VICTORIA OFFICE:

Bank of Montreal Building,   ·   ·   Victoria, B. C.

February, B.C. Electric opened its car building shops, under the direction of Thomas Driscoll, in New Westminster, and its very first products, cars 24, 25 and 26, single-truckers, were assigned to Victoria.

By the end of May 1904, the company regarded Rock Bay Bridge and the seven blocks of track on Store Street as superfluous. Through March and April, track laying had progressed on Government Street between Johnson and Bay streets, and also on the three blocks of Bay Street between Government and Bridge streets, at the north end of Rock Bay Bridge. Furthermore, a new Point Ellice Bridge, to last fifty-three years, had been opened on April 18.

On Friday, May 5, 1905, when track and overhead wire were in place as far as Tillicum Road, a half-hourly shuttle streetcar service over Victoria's first new line in years, the Gorge line, began operating from the Esquimalt line. This new 1.61-mile thrust opened for through service on May 15, culminating in the system's first loop, at the Gorge.

The long-awaited opening of B.C. Electric's Gorge Park occurred on July 26, and on August 23, B.C. Electric inaugurated a sightseeing service, with open car 20 operating twice a day from the corner of Yates and Government streets to the Gorge, Esquimalt, and Oak Bay. At this time of increasing public interest in the expanding system, Johannes Buntzen had left for London on July 1 to become chairman of the board of B.C. Electric. The new general manager was Rochfort Henry Sperling.

A petition spurred the company to rebuild the track at the north end of Douglas Street abandoned eight years previously, extending it at the same time to Cloverdale Avenue; part of the Outer Wharf run, the new section was opened for service on November 27, 1906. On July 26, B.C. Electric's office staff had moved into its commodious new building at 1016 Langley Street. Designed by Rattenbury, the two-storey brick structure was a relief from the outgrown quarters at 25 Yates Street.

For most, the best news of 1906 was the arrival from New Westminster in May of streetcars 70 and 71, the very first of the large double-trucked vehicles which almost immediately marked the single-truckers for obsolescence. In 1907, a Rattenbury designed 60-by-120-foot Pembroke Streetcar barn addition was completed.

On January 3, 1908, Victoria had experienced its first streetcar–automobile accident, at Victoria's busiest intersection, even today, Douglas and Yates streets. Although the automobile was destroyed, the *Colonist* insisted that "the street car suffered no injuries worth mentioning." With the opening of the Empress Hotel on January 20, Victoria gained a world-class facility, one in whose construction B.C. Electric had played a significant role, having run a spur onto its site for conveying gravel and fill.

Although a new streetcar line was begun on May 28, "from a juncture with the Willows car line at the corner of the Cadboro Bay and Richmond roads, to Mount Tolmie, a distance of a mile and three quarters,"[24] it was not initially conceived as a streetcar line, but rather a means by which Arthur Lineham of Lineham Sand & Gravel Company could service his four-million-cubic-yard sand and gravel pit at Mount Tolmie.

In early August the company announced a contemplated new line – never built – "to loop Gorge line by connecting up with the Outer Wharf and Douglas street line at the junction of Douglas and Government streets."[25] Recently arrived streetcar 75 was involved in an experiment on November 3 which turned out to be a complete success, and had important ramifications for the whole streetcar fleet: fitted with air brakes, the car demonstrated their effectiveness, leading to their installation on all the other double-trucked cars.[26]

The new cemetery-Foul Bay streetcar began service with car 107 at 9 a.m. on March 21, 1909, ending in a loop to the north of Fairfield Road at Foul Bay Road.[27] More new trackage was inaugurated with the opening of the racing season at the Willows on June 5, with a large loop off Cadboro Bay Road occupying Eastdowne Road, Fair Street, and Epworth Street.[28]

It was on Saturday evening, May 23, that B.C. Electric in Victoria had been involved in its first fatality, the victim a fifteen-year-old boy, struck down by car 118 on Fort Street at Quadra. Although his death was ruled accidental, a recommendation came that far-side-of-the-street stops should be supplanted by near-side halting points.[29]

A new observation car, 123, another New Westminster product, described by the *Colonist* as having "seats arranged in tiers, one rising above the other, without a canopy and entered from the rear, with an aisle down the centre,"[30] went into service on July 11, with two daily three-hour trips; the fare was fifty cents, and a wye had been installed at the Esquimalt terminus for car 123, as well as for recently arrived single-ended streetcars 117 - 122.

B.C. Electric installed a large clock for its employees in June 1910 at the crucial corner of Yates and Douglas streets, and on July 9, car 183, the first of six new PAYE cars (pay as you enter) arrived, followed shortly by 184 - 188, going into regular service on Douglas–Outer Wharf and Gorge.

At the same time that the V. & S. was withdrawing, in a sense – its new and last depot opened on December 20 on the west side of Blanshard Street between Herald and Fisgard streets[31] – B.C. Electric was moving to create an interurban line within Saanich, the

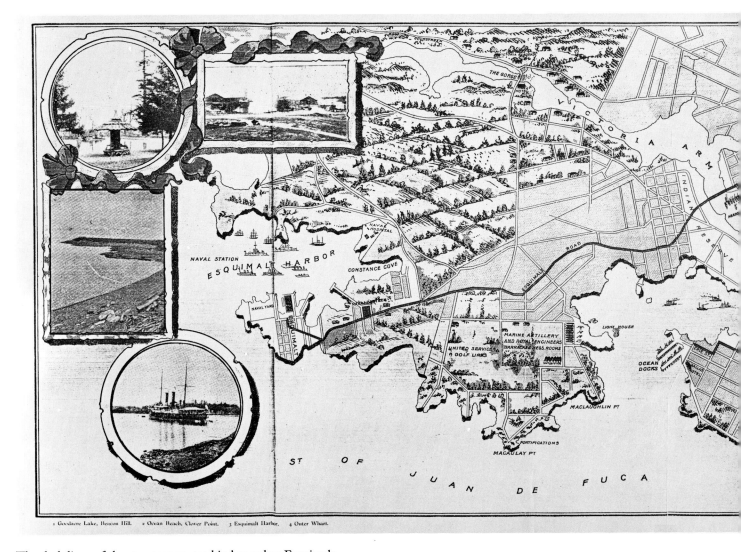

1 Goodacre Lake, Beacon Hill.   2 Ocean Beach, Clover Point.   3 Esquimalt Harbor.   4 Outer Wharf.

The dark lines of the streetcar routes bind together Esquimalt,
the City of Victoria, and Oak Bay at the turn of the century.

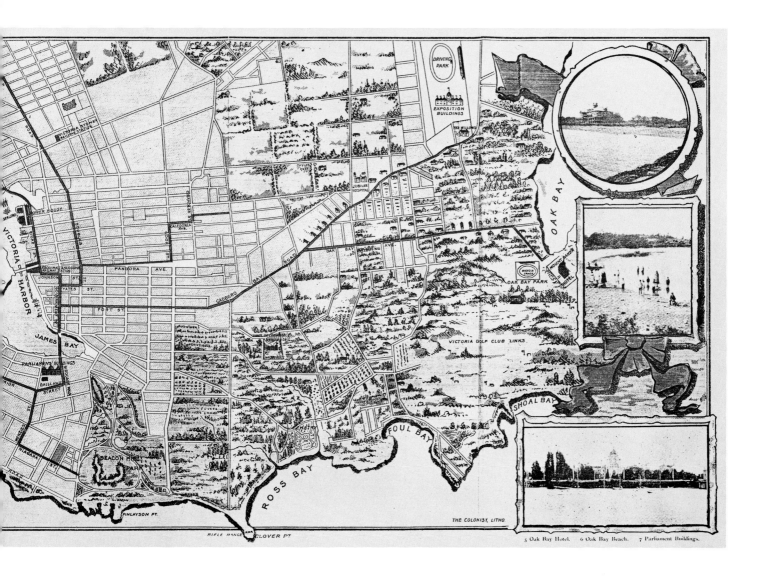

5 Oak Bay Hotel.   6 Oak Bay Beach.   7 Parliament Buildings.

PARLIAMENT BUILDINGS.

The handsomest pile of public buildings in America should not escape the Tourist's eye. Cars every ten minutes.

❖❖❖❖❖❖

OAK BAY.

Take the Fort Street Car—fare is Five Cents and the time involved not more than twenty minutes travel each way. **The Royal Jubilee Hospital** and **Victoria Driving Park** are passed *en route*.

The lovely view to be obtained of Mount Baker and Mount Rainier on a clear day, as well as of the beautiful bay studded with its green little islets, will amply repay the visitor.

The Victoria Golf Club Links on Gonzales Point are distant a short ten minutes walk.

The MOUNT BAKER HOTEL, a famous Summer Resort, will at reasonable prices provide the "inner man" with refreshments.

❖❖❖❖❖❖

The Oak Bay Recreation Grounds

—WITH ITS EXCELLENT—

BICYCLE TRACK,

pronounced the finest on the Pacific Coast, and **Athletic Grounds,** are close by the terminus, and an attraction of sorts will usually afford the visitor some amusement.

Band Concerts are given at the Mount Baker Hotel during the summer in the evenings.

British Columbia Electric Railway Co.

→LIMITED,←

···OPERATING···

STREET RAILWAYS

IN THE CITIES OF

VICTORIA,——

VANCOUVER AND

WESTMINSTER,

- AND BETWEEN -

VICTORIA & ESQUIMALT

- AND -

VANCOUVER & WESTMINSTER

VICTORIA BRANCH

BRITISH COLUMBIA
ELECTRIC RAILWAY COMPANY, Limited.
Pass **1909** CANCELLED.
OVER VICTORIA LINES
Until 31st December, 1909, unless otherwise ordered.
No. 1015
THIS PASS MUST ALWAYS BE SHOWN TO CONDUCTOR
General Manager.

Car 22 in 1901, splendidly new and still with only one trolley pole, swung from one end to the other, far out on Fort Street.   RONALD A. GREENE COLLECTION

(left) Armature room, traffic superintendent H. Gibson on the right.
RONALD A. GREENE COLLECTION

(right) Lighting room, Gibson, third from right.
RONALD A. GREENE COLLECTION

R. P. Rithet's Outer Wharf complex, with one of the new, large double-truck streetcars. Notice the Outer Wharf streetcar line's terminal shelter, emblazoned with "CARS to CITY."
VICTORIA CITY ARCHIVES

It's springtime 1909, and two new streetcars, 120 and 121, resplendently green with gold trim, have arrived in Victoria, soon to be in service with their running mate, the first Foul Bay car, 107, in the distance.
RONALD A. GREENE COLLECTION

Sightseeing car 123 in summer 1909, making its very first swing through the streetcar system, poses momentarily at Esquimalt.
RONALD A. GREENE COLLECTION

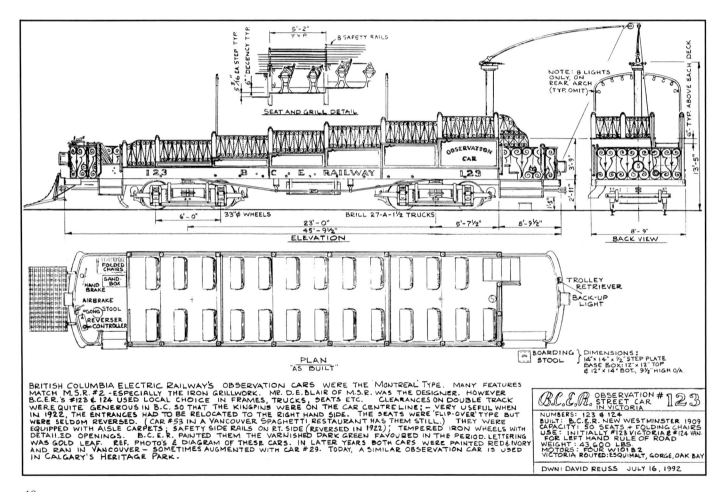

SEAT AND GRILL DETAIL

8 SAFETY RAILS

5'-2" TYP.

6" DECENCY TYP.

3½" EA STEP TYP.

OBSERVATION CAR

NOTE: 8 LIGHTS ONLY, ON REAR ARCH (TYP. OMIT)

6" TYP. ABOVE EACH DECK

13'-5"

3'-9"

2'-11"

123   B. C. E. RAILWAY   123

6'-0"   33"∅ WHEELS   BRILL 27-A-1½ TRUCKS   5'-7½"   5'-9½"

23'-0"

45'-9½"

ELEVATION

8'-9"

BACK VIEW

PLAN
"AS BUILT"

FOLDED CHAIRS

SAND BOX

HAND BRAKE

AIRBRAKE

GONG   STOOL

REVERSER

CONTROLLER

TROLLEY RETRIEVER

BACK-UP LIGHT

BOARDING STOOL

DIMENSIONS:
14"x14"x½" STEP PLATE
BASE BOX: 12"x12" TOP
& 12"x14" BOT. 9½" HIGH O/A

BRITISH COLUMBIA ELECTRIC RAILWAY'S OBSERVATION CARS WERE THE MONTREAL TYPE. MANY FEATURES MATCH M.S.R. #2 - ESPECIALLY THE IRON GRILLWORK. MR. D.E.BLAIR OF M.S.R. WAS THE DESIGNER. HOWEVER B.C.E.R.'s #123 & 124 USED LOCAL CHOICE IN FRAMES, TRUCKS, SEATS ETC. CLEARANCES ON DOUBLE TRACK WERE QUITE GENEROUS IN B.C. SO THAT THE KINGPINS WERE ON THE CAR CENTRE LINE; - VERY USEFUL WHEN IN 1922, THE ENTRANCES HAD TO BE RELOCATED TO THE RIGHT HAND SIDE. THE SEATS WERE 'FLIP-OVER' TYPE BUT WERE SELDOM REVERSED. (CAR #53 IN A VANCOUVER SPAGHETTI RESTAURANT HAS THEM STILL.) THEY WERE EQUIPPED WITH AISLE CARPETS; SAFETY SIDE RAILS ON RT. SIDE (REVERSED IN 1922); TEMPERED IRON WHEELS WITH DETAILED OPENINGS. B.C.E.R. PAINTED THEM THE VARNISHED DARK GREEN FAVOURED IN THE PERIOD. LETTERING WAS GOLD LEAF. REF. PHOTO'S & DIAGRAM OF THESE CARS. IN LATER YEARS BOTH CARS WERE PAINTED RED & IVORY AND RAN IN VANCOUVER — SOMETIMES AUGMENTED WITH CAR #29. TODAY, A SIMILAR OBSERVATION CAR IS USED IN CALGARY'S HERITAGE PARK.

B.C.E.R. OBSERVATION STREET CAR #123
IN VICTORIA

NUMBERS: 123 & 124
BUILT: B.C.E.R. NEW WESTMINSTER 1909
CAPACITY: 50 SEATS + FOLDING CHAIRS
USE: INITIALLY #123 VICTORIA & #124 VAN.
FOR LEFT HAND RULE OF ROAD
WEIGHT: 43,600 LBS.
MOTORS: FOUR W101 B2
VICTORIA ROUTED: ESQUIMALT, GORGE, OAK BAY

DWN: DAVID REUSS   JULY 16, 1992

Observation car 123's second summer of operation featured three complete daily circuits.
H. R. HALLS COLLECTION

LOAD CAPACITIES OF CITY PASSENGER CARS. AUTHORIZED BY INSPECTOR RAE.														
CAR NUMBERS	TYPE			DIMENSIONS				AREAS SQ. FT.			CAPACITY				% STANDING CAPACITY OF SEATING
	PAYE	STYLE	MAKE	BODY	PLATFORM		TOTAL	SEATS	STAND'G	TOTAL	SEATS	AISLE	PL'FRM	TOTAL	
					FRONT	REAR									
DOUBLE END 11	NO	OPEN	BRILL	21'-0"	4'-1¼	4'-1¼	29·3	165	12	177	50	0	3	53	6
1-6, 8,9,27,30,	NO	CLOSED	SHOPS	20'-0"	5'-0"	5'-0"	30·0	112	57·9	169·9	28	9	5	42	50
7, 26.	NO	"	"	22'-6"	4'-9"	4'-9"	32·0	118·25	75·4	193·65	32	14	5	51	59·4
12, 13.	NO	"	BRILL	24'-6"	4'-9"	4'-9"	34·0	112·8	77	189·8	32	13	5	50	56·3
22, 23.	NO	"	OTTAWA	29'-0"	5'-6"	5'-6"	40·0	162·4	83·7	246·1	44	13	5	62	41
69-71, 73,107.	NO	"	SHOPS	30'-0"	6'-1⅞	6'-1⅞	42·3⅜	174	91·75	265·75	48	14	5	67	39·6
183-188, 231-234, 237-239	YES	SEMI-CONV.	SHOPS	31'-10"	7'-0"	7'-0"	45·10	138	136·6	274·6	40	20	7	67	67·5
193-194.	YES	"	"	30-6¼	7'-0"	7'-0"	44·6¾	145	104	249	36	21	5	62	72·25
SINGLE END. 117-122.	YES	CLOSED	SHOPS	30'-3	6'-6"	7'-3"	44·0	167·8	104·7	272·5	48	14	7	69	43·8
250-255.	YES	"	"	31'-10"	5'-2"	7'-6"	44·6	145·5	134·5	280	45	20	8	73	62·3
FEB. 26th 1913 FBR.					VICTORIA B·C·								Gnd Tripp ENG. SUP'T.		

Filed in 1913, a few weeks after the inauguration of Victoria's last streetcar line, Tripp's report cites 49 vehicles available for service.
AUTHOR'S COLLECTION

Locomotive 905 in a rare,
early pose, with a body considerably altered
in later years.
ROBERT TURNER COLLECTION

Victoria Day celebrations at Gorge Park
were always the prelude to summer.   PABC

The splendid Willows exhibition
and race track facilities.
PABC

Car 236 sports the company's
racy green, white and gold
paint scheme while servicing
Beacon Hill–Fernwood.   PABC

territory of the Victoria & Sidney. The precise route of this 22.96-mile line had been established in November, selected from three potential routes surveyed over a seven-month period by company civil engineer C. Hoard.

On March 1, 1911, a railway ministry having been established by B.C.'s government, "tramway" rules came into effect, bolstered by a 120-page booklet of rules and regulations. Six months later, the greater Victoria area received its first electricity from B.C. Electric's new 3,200-kilowatt generator at Jordan River, some thirty-five miles west of Victoria.

Boldly coloured sheet-metal signs, diagonally marked and with destination indicated, hung on either side of a streetcar's headlight; coloured lights at each end of the car's roof identified its destination for its night-riding passengers. In 1911, the various lines displayed their orientation in the following fashion: Beacon Hill–Fernwood, green signs and one green light; Douglas–Outer Wharf, white signs and one white light; Esquimalt, red signs and one red light; Foul Bay, green and white signs, and green and white lights; Gorge, green signs and two green lights; Oak Bay, red and white signs, and red and white lights; and Willows, red signs and two red lights.

The Dominion-wide census in 1911 revealed Victoria's population to be 31,660, and the opening of Canada's first artificial ice arena, a splendid 4,200-seat facility at the northeast corner of Cadboro Bay Road and Epworth Street costing $110,000, confirmed the excellence of the province's economy in the Victoria area.

Temporary streetcar service commenced in mid-March of 1912 on the completed section of Burnside Road, the new Saanich interurban line's exit route from Victoria. In addition, the presence of University School (present-day Camosun College) along the

---

BRITISH COLUMBIA ELECTRIC RAILWAY CO., LTD.

VICTORIA BRANCH

TIME TABLE

DECEMBER
1911

	WEEK DAYS	SUNDAYS
OAK BAY *Cars show Red and White light, and Red and White signs.*		
First Car leaves Government St. — Oak Bay	6.00 A.M. / 6.20 "	9.00 A.M. / 9.20 "
Last Car leaves Government St. — Oak Bay	11.40 P.M. / 12.00 "	10.40 A.M. / 11.00 "
6.00 A.M. to 11.40 A.M. / 8.00 P.M. to 11.40 P.M. — Cars every 20 minutes		
11.40 A.M. to 8.00 P.M. — Cars every 10 minutes		
Sundays, Cars every 10 minutes		
WILLOWS *Cars show two Red lights, and Red signs.*		
First Car leaves Government St. — Willows	5.50 A.M. / 6.10 "	8.50 A.M. / 9.10 "
Last Car leaves Government St. — Willows	11.30 P.M. / 11.50 "	10.30 P.M. / 10.50 "
5.50 A.M. to 11.45 A.M. / 8.10 P.M. to 11.30 P.M. — Cars every 20 minutes		Saturdays, 10 minute service extended to 10.30 p.m.
11.45 A.M. to 8.10 P.M. — Cars every 10 minutes		
Sundays, Cars every 20 minutes		
ESQUIMALT *Cars show One Red light, and Red signs.*		
First Car leaves Government St. — Esquimalt	6.00 A.M. / 6.22½ "	9.00 A.M. / 9.22½ "
Last Car leaves Government St. — Esquimalt	11.45 P.M. / 12.07½ "	10.45 P.M. / 11.07½ "
Cars every 15 minutes		
GORGE *Cars show Two Green lights, and Green signs.*		
First Car leaves Government St. — Gorge	6.07½ A.M. / 6.15 "	9.07½ A.M. / 9.15 "
Last Car leaves Government St. — Gorge	11.37½ P.M. / 12.00 "	10.37½ P.M. / 11.00 "
6.07½ A.M. to 2.20 P.M. — Cars every 15 minutes		
2.20 P.M. to 10.30 P.M. — Cars every 10		
FOUL BAY *Cars show Green and White lights, and Green and White signs.*		
First Car leaves Government St. — Foul Bay	5.52½ A.M. / 6.15 "	8.52½ A.M. / 9.15 "
Last Car leaves Government St. — Foul Bay	11.37½ P.M. / 12.00 "	10.37½ P.M. / 11.00 "
Cars every 15 minutes		

PRICE OF TICKETS

6 Green Tickets	25c.	Obtainable on all Cars. Unlimited.
8 White "	25c.	Limited
25 Red "	$1.00	Unlimited
10 School "	25c.	{ at Langley or Government Street Ticket Office.

BEACON HILL	WEEK DAYS	SUNDAYS
Cars show One Green light, and Green signs.		
First Car leaves Government St. Beacon Hill	6.00 A.M. 6.10 "	9.00 A.M. 9.10 "
Last Car leaves Government St. Beacon Hill	11.30 P.M. 11.40 "	10.30 P.M. 10.40 "
Cars every 10 minutes		
SPRING RIDGE		
Cars show One Green light, and Green signs.		
First Car leaves Government St. Spring Ridge	6.00 A.M. 6.10 "	9.00 A.M. 9.10 "
Last Car leaves Government St. Spring Ridge	11.30 P.M. 11.40 "	10.30 P.M. 10.40 "
Cars every 10 minutes		
OUTER WHARF		
Cars show One White light, and White signs.		
First Car leaves Government St. Outer Wharf	6.00 A.M. 6.12 "	9.00 A.M. 9.12 "
Last Car leaves Government St. Outer Wharf	11.36 P.M. 11.48 "	10.36 P.M. 10.48 "
Cars every 12 minutes		
CLOVERDALE		
Cars show One White light, and White signs.		
First Car leaves Government St. Cloverdale	6.00 A.M. 6.12 "	9.00 A.M. 9.12 "
Last Car leaves Government St. Cloverdale	11.36 P.M. 11.48 "	10.36 P.M. 10.48 "
Cars every 12 minutes		

UNIVERSITY SCHOOL CAR
Mount Tolmie
Car leaves Government St. 7.30 A.M. 8.10 A.M. and 4.30 P.M.
Saturday 8.50 A.M. Car omitted.   Cars not running Sundays.

OBSERVATION CAR
During Summer Months only.

This Time Table may be Changed at any Time Without Notice.

Mount Tolmie line had persuaded B.C. Electric to institute a limited streetcar service for the school's students and staff.

In early August, a code of rules promulgated by B.C.'s attorney general, Hon. W. J. Bowser, under the authority of the Tramway Inspection Act, arrived on the desks of company officials, citing thirty-six points which needed immediate attention: streetcars had to be equipped with doors or gates, cars had to be standardized, wire mesh window screens had to be installed, etc. As if the new code of rules was not enough of a shock, what must B.C. Electric officials have thought when, on August 12, Victoria aldermen Cuthbert, Gleason, and Porter were appointed by city council "to secure data as to the feasibility of inaugurating a municipal owned system of motor buses in the city to provide more adequate accommodation for passenger traffic for certain sections of the city, at present unserved by the B.C.E. company's lines."? The idea was Cuthbert's, and nothing came of it.[32]

On September 23, Burnside Road received regular streetcar service from its western terminus at Washington Avenue, and on December 2, regular streetcar service was begun on the new 5,720-foot, double-tracked Hillside line, Douglas Street to Cedar Hill Road, with streetcars looping downtown via Government and Douglas streets, and displaying large red and green destination signs. Ten days later construction began on a third floor for the head office building at Fort and Langley. Put in place during the year had been a short streetcar line extension on Cook Street north from the Fernwood line to Royal Athletic Park.

Exactly 10,976,208 riders had graced Victoria's streetcars during 1912, 65,581,267 on B.C. Electric's complete system, on 281 cars. Of the company's 258.77 miles of line, 134.21 were interurban run (Chilliwack line, 72.42; Lulu Island line, 33.21; Central Park line, 18.52; and Burnaby Lake line, 10.06) and 124.56 were streetcar run (greater Vancouver, 77.43; greater Victoria, 28.95; North Vancouver, 10.63; and New Westminster, 7.55).

On February 2, 1913, the 7,570-foot Uplands line went into service, from the Willows to its graceful loop on Midland Circle, via Cadboro Bay Road, and Dalhousie and Dunlevy streets, which became Midlands Road within Uplands subdivision, whose parent, Uplands Limited, had contributed $1,817.13 to the last half-mile of the line, which had its own private right of way and attractive ornamental trolley wire hangers. Uplands destination signs were emblazoned with an orange circle on a red background.

On May 3, a contract was awarded for the construction of "the Burnside–Cloverdale branch," a looping line from Burnside Road (near Harriet Road) via Irma Street and Ardersier Road east to Douglas Street (and a new car barn soon to be completed on Cloverdale Avenue).[33] This line would not be built.

The next new line was announced on May 5, "the Bay extension," which would run on Quadra Street from Pandora Avenue, then east on Bay Street to Shelbourne Street, where a substantial streetcar barn would be erected.[34] Although the line would not be built – the Uplands line would be the last – the two-track turn-off onto Quadra Street from Pandora Avenue was for years a reminder of what might have been.

For use on the Saanich interurban line, six new steel interurban cars, lavatory equipped, numbers 1239 - 1244; an express car, number 1706; and a forty-eight-ton steel locomotive, 981, had arrived from the St. Louis Car Company, Niles Car and Manufacturing Company, and Baldwin Locomotive Works, respectively. (The six St. Louis cars had been ordered initially by Pacific Northwest Traction for its new interurban line south from Bellingham, Wash-

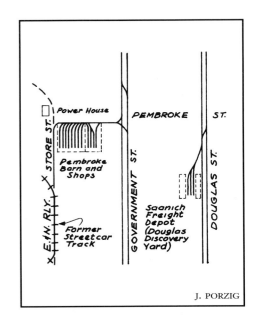

54

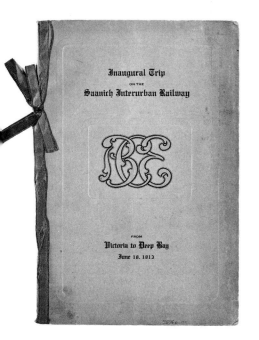

ington.) These vehicles had arrived at Sidney by sea, to be brought by the V. & S. to Saanichton, where an interchange line with the B.C. Electric line had been laid; from there it was a fifteen-mile run into Victoria. (Car 1706's twin, 1707, also made a brief appearance, only to be shipped back to Vancouver on September 27.)

On June 18, the Saanich interurban line was opened with splendid fanfare as about one hundred guests rode out onto Douglas Street from a new depot at 11:25 a.m. on a train consisting of cars 1706, 1240 and 1242, in that order, decked out in colourful bunting and flags. (The depot was the former Pythian Castle Hall, at the northeast corner of Pandora Avenue and Douglas Street; "Cormorant yard" was the designation of the three-track depot compound behind the building itself.)

In bright sunlight just after 12:30 p.m. at Deep Bay, the northern terminus, British Columbia's premier, Hon. Sir Richard McBride, drove the ceremonial last spike, calling "for three times three and a tiger for the B.C. Electric Company."

On the return journey, following an outdoor luncheon, a stop was made at the end of the short Patricia Bay spur, as well as at the half-way point of the line for guests to inspect the company's new Brentwood steam plant, imposing with its huge stack, on the line's west side. At 4:30 p.m. the crew of four brought the inaugural party back to the Victoria depot: conductor F. Clutterbuck, motorman G. Rhodes, and brakemen J. W. Jackson and R. A. Robertson.

Painted a sparkling dark green with brown trim, and matching gold lettering and numbering, as well as with a gold decorative line running the full lengths of the cars, the seven interurban coaches were an especially attractive sight as they inaugurated regular service on the following day.

The Saanich line was a state-of-the-art interurban line, one which had not come cheaply at $910,563. In addition to the Patricia Bay spur, another spur would soon be in place to Tod Inlet; more than a year earlier, an enormous gravel pit, still an impressive sight today, had been established at the end of a mile-long spur turning south, east of Sluggetts, at Pit Junction. The only other spur of note along the line was the turnout at Harriet Road, north off Burnside Road. Freight runs operated from a new three-track freight depot, "Douglas Discovery yard," three blocks north of Cormorant Street on the west side of Douglas Street between Chatham and Discovery streets.[35]

By August 22, Victoria's streetcar system was entirely PAYE; the company perceived two key gains: greater safety, as the conductor need never leave his position, and better time, crews tending to keep PAYE cars more tightly on schedule. On July 23, limited but regular streetcar service had been initiated on the Mount Tolmie line, directly to and from downtown. In mid-September, a new car barn had been opened, off Cloverdale Avenue, east of the north end of Douglas Street. Along with yard tracks, the wooden-framed, corrugated iron barn measured 384 feet by 38 feet, covering two tracks and sixteen streetcars, planned to house those from the Burnside, Esquimalt, and Hillside lines.

In mid-October B.C. Electric, in conjunction with West Coast Development, initiated a ferry service from Deep Bay with the forty-four-passenger *Enilada*, connecting with the interurban trains to Beaver Point, Burgoyne, Fulford Harbour, Maple Bay, Moresby Island, Portland Island, Port Washington, and Vesuvius. Too little business ended the ferry service before year's end.

Riders of the Foul Bay line were particularly encouraged by the increase of service frequency on November 1, attributable to

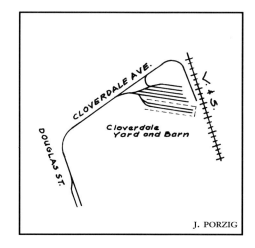

J. PORZIG

Cloverdale Yard and Barn

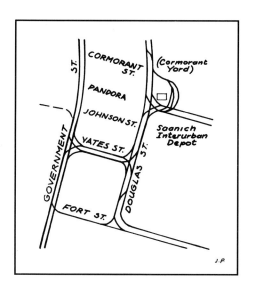

the newly constructed siding at Arnold Avenue, alongside the cemetery.

April 2, 1914 witnessed the inauguration of interlocking gates at Russells, just west of Springfield Street on Esquimalt Road, the only B.C. Electric grade crossing on the Victoria system with a steam railway, the E. & N.[36] Two days later, ten, new, double-ended, PAYE streetcars, numbers 381 - 390, costing $7,500 each, arrived from Preston Car and Coach Company in Ontario.

Rochfort Henry Sperling had been promoted to the position of assistant to Horne-Payne in London in late March, and George Kidd became B.C. Electric's new general manager on May 6. It was the same day on which the company announced that a tea-room and twenty-three-bedroom hotel, The Chalet, would be constructed at Deep Bay. Within a few short weeks, B.C. Electric's "own" Frank Stillman Barnard would take up residence at Government House in Victoria as British Columbia's Lieutenant-Governor.

Sidney residents, not happy with their mile-long walk to the Saanich line (Sidney had been legally off-limits to B.C. Electric, its precincts belonging to the G.N.-operated V. & S.), acquired a bus service of sorts from an A. L. Allison in mid-June, when he began making two trips daily, with a fifty-cent fare, to Victoria in his five-passenger vehicle.

B.C. Electric extended itself continually in an effort to make the Saanich line financially viable, even to inaugurating the "Brentwood Limited" and the "Brentwood Flyer" on July 7, special trains from Victoria to the recently-opened Brentwood Hotel, with its beautiful view over Tod and Saanich inlets. Market specials, with car 1706, between Saanichton and Victoria were tried but dropped for want of patronage. In mid-October, interurban car 1501 was seen for the first time on the Saanich line; it had seating for thirty passengers,

Weekday service on the Saanich line at the inauguration of one-man service on May 27, 1923.
AUTHOR'S COLLECTION

WEEK DAYS. NORTHBOUND—Read Down

Zone Number	Fare From Victoria	Statn. Number	Miles From Victoria	STATIONS	A.M.	A.M.	A.M.	A.M.	A.M.	A.M.	A.M.	A.M.	A.M.	P.M.	P.M.	P.M.	P.M.	P.M.	P.M.	P.M.	P.M.	P.M.	P.M.	P.M.	P.M.
1	.05	1	.0	VICTORIA	6.55	7.00	7.55	8.00		9.35	10.00	11.00	11.50	1.30	1.35	1.40	3.30	4.30	4.35	5.30	5.35	6.30	7.30	8.30	11.30
	.05	2	1.9	HARRIETT	7.04	7.09	8.04	8.09	9.09	9.44	10.09	11.09	12.00	1.39	1.44	1.49	3.39	4.39	4.44	5.39	5.44	6.39	7.39	8.39	11.39
	.05	3	2.3	BURNSIDE RD. Way Pts.	7.05	7.10	8.05	8.10	9.10	9.45	10.10	11.10	12.01	1.40	1.45	1.50	3.40	4.40	4.45	5.40	5.46	6.40	7.40	8.40	11.40
2	.10	4	2.6	TILLICUM	7.06	7.13	8.08	8.13	9.11	9.47	10.13	11.13	12.04	1.43	1.48	1.53	3.43	4.43	4.48	5.43	5.48	6.43	7.43	8.43	11.43
	.10	5	3.4	MARIGOLD	7.08	7.16	8.11	8.16	9.13	9.49	10.16	11.16	12.07	1.46	1.51	1.56	3.46	4.46	4.51	5.46	5.51	6.46	7.46	8.46	11.46
3	.15	6	3.8	BLACKWOOD ROAD	7.10	7.18	8.13	8.18	9.15	9.51	10.18	11.18	12.09	1.48	1.53	1.58	3.48	4.48	4.53	5.48	5.53	6.48	7.48	8.48	11.48
	.15	7	4.3	WILKINSON	7.12	7.19	8.14	8.19	9.17	9.53	10.19	11.19	12.10	1.49	1.54	1.59	3.49	4.49	4.54	5.49	5.54	6.49	7.49	8.49	11.49
	.15	8	4.8	GLYN	7.13	7.21	8.16	8.21	9.18	9.55	10.21	11.21	12.12	1.51	1.56	2.01	3.51	4.51	4.56	5.51	5.56	6.51	7.51	8.51	11.51
	.15	9	5.4	EBERTS	7.15	7.24	8.19	8.24	9.20	9.57	10.24	11.24	12.15	1.54	1.59	2.04	3.54	4.54	4.59	5.54	5.59	6.54	7.54	8.54	11.54
4	.20	10	6.2	WESTWOODVALE		7.27		8.27		10.00	10.27	11.27	12.18	1.57	2.02	2.07	3.57	4.57	5.02	5.57	6.02	7.06	8.02	8.59	11.57
	.20	11	6.7	GOWARD		7.29		8.29		10.02	10.29	11.29	12.20	1.59	2.04	2.09	3.59	4.59	5.04	5.59	6.04	7.08	8.04	9.01	11.59
	.20	12	7.4	OBSERVATORY		7.31		8.31		10.04	10.31	11.31	12.22	2.01	4.01	5.01	5.06	6.01	6.06	7.10	8.06	9.03	12.01		
5	.25	13	7.9	PROSPECT		7.32		8.32		10.05	10.32	11.32	12.23	2.02	2.07	2.12	4.02	5.02	5.07	6.02	6.07	7.11	8.07	9.04	12.02
	.25	14	8.9	HEALS		7.34		8.34		10.07	10.34	11.34	12.25	2.04	2.09	2.14	4.04	5.04	5.09	6.04	6.09	7.13	8.09	9.06	12.04
6	.30	15	9.7	RIFLE RANGE		7.37		8.37			10.37	11.37	12.28	2.07	2.12	2.17	4.07	5.07	5.12	6.07	6.12	7.16	8.12	9.09	12.07
	.30	16	10.2	DURRANCE		7.38		8.38			10.38	11.38	12.29	2.08	2.13	2.18	4.08	5.08	5.13	6.08	6.13	7.17	8.13	9.10	12.08
7	.35	17	11.2	TODD INLET		7.40		8.40			10.40	11.40	12.31	2.10	2.15	2.20	4.10	5.10	5.15	6.10	6.15	7.19	8.15	9.12	12.10
	.35	18	11.6	BRENTWOOD		7.41		8.41			10.41	11.41	12.32	2.11	2.16	2.21	4.11	5.11	5.16	6.11	6.16	7.20	8.16	9.13	12.11
	.35	19	12.2	MARCHANT ROAD		7.43		8.43			10.43	11.43	12.34	2.13	2.18	2.23	4.13	5.13	5.18	6.13	6.18	7.22	8.18	9.15	12.13
	.35	20	12.5	SLUGGETTS		7.44		8.44			10.44	11.44	12.35	2.14	2.19	2.24	4.14	5.14	5.19	6.14	6.19	7.24	8.20	9.17	12.14
8	.40	21	13.6	STELLYS		7.47		8.47			10.47	11.47		2.17	2.22		4.17	5.17	5.22	6.17		7.27	8.23	9.20	12.17
	.40	22	14.2	PROSSER AVENUE		7.48		8.48			10.48	11.48		2.18	2.23		4.18	5.18	5.23	6.18		7.28	8.24	9.21	12.18
	.40	22	14.9	SAANICHTON		7.50		8.50			10.50	11.50		2.20	2.25		4.20	5.20	5.25	6.20		7.30	8.26	9.23	12.20
9	.50	23	16.9	EXPERIMENTAL FARM				8.56				11.55		2.25			5.25							9.28	
	.50	24	17.4	BAZAN BAY				8.58				11.57		2.27			5.27							9.30	
	.50	25	17.8	TRIPP				9.00				11.58		2.28			5.28							9.31	
	.50	26	18.8	SIDNEWAY				9.03				12.01		2.31			5.31							9.34	
10	.60	27	19.4	MEADLANDS				9.05				12.03		2.33			5.33							9.36	
	.60	28	19.8	GIBSON'S CROSSING				9.07				12.05		2.35			5.35							9.38	
11	.65	29	20.9	MALLOWMOT				9.10				12.09		2.39			5.39							9.39	
	.65	30	22.3	TATLOW				9.14				12.13		2.43			5.43							9.43	
	.65	31	23.0	DEEP BAY				9.20				12.15		2.50			5.50							9.50	
					A.M.	A.M.	A.M.	A.M.	A.M.	A.M.	A.M.	A.M.	P.M.	P.M.	P.M.	P.M.	P.M.	P.M.	P.M.	P.M.	P.M.	P.M.	P.M.	P.M.	A.M.

WEEK DAYS. SOUTHBOUND—Read Up.

Zone Number	Fare From Victoria	Statn. Number	Miles From Victoria	STATIONS	A.M.	A.M.	A.M.	A.M.	A.M.	A.M.	A.M.	A.M.	P.M.	P.M.	P.M.	P.M.	P.M.	P.M.	P.M.	P.M.	P.M.	P.M.	P.M.	P.M.	A.M.
1		1	.0	VICTORIA	7.50	8.50	8.55		9.50	10.50	10.55	11.50	1.30	1.35	3.20	4.20	4.25	5.25	6.25	7.20	7.25	9.20	11.20	1.20
	.05	2	1.9	HARRIETT	7.36	8.36	8.41	9.40	10.40	10.45	11.40	1.21	1.26	3.10	4.10	4.15	5.15	6.15	7.10	7.15	7.20	8.16	9.11	11.10	1.10
	.05	3	2.3	BURNSIDE RD. Way Pts.	7.36	8.36	8.41	9.36	10.36	10.41	11.36	1.17	1.22	3.06	4.06	4.11	5.11	6.11	7.06	7.11	7.16	8.12	9.08	11.06	1.06
2	.10	4	2.6	TILLICUM	7.35	8.35	8.40	9.35	10.35	10.40	11.35	1.16	1.21	3.05	4.05	4.10	5.10	6.10	7.05	7.10	7.15	8.10	9.05	11.05	1.05
	.10	5	3.4	MARIGOLD	7.32	8.32	8.37	9.32	10.32	10.37	11.32	1.13	1.18	3.02	4.02	4.07	5.07	6.07	7.02	7.07	7.12	8.08	9.05	11.02	1.02
3	.15	6	3.8	BLACKWOOD ROAD	7.30	8.30	8.35	9.30	10.30	10.35	11.30	1.11	1.16	3.00	4.00	4.05	5.05	6.05	7.00	7.05	7.10	8.06	9.03	11.00	1.00
	.15	7	4.3	WILKINSON	7.29	8.29	8.34	9.29	10.29	10.34	11.29	1.10	1.15	2.59	3.59	4.04	5.04	6.04	6.59	7.04	7.09	8.05	9.02	10.59	12.59
	.15	8	4.8	GLYN	7.27	8.27	8.32	9.27	10.27	10.32	11.27	1.08	1.13	2.57	3.57	4.02	5.02	6.02	6.57	7.02	7.07	8.03	9.00	10.57	12.57
	.15	9	5.4	EBERTS	7.24	8.24	8.28	9.25	10.24	10.29	11.24	1.05	1.10	2.54	3.54	3.59	4.54	5.54	6.54	6.59	7.04	8.00	8.57	10.54	12.54
4	.20	10	6.2	WESTWOODVALE		8.21			10.21	10.26	11.21	1.02	1.07	2.51	3.51	3.56	4.51	5.51	6.51	6.56	7.01	7.58	8.54	10.51	12.51
	.20	11	6.7	GOWARD		8.19			10.19	10.24	11.19	1.00	1.05	2.49	3.49	3.54	4.49	5.49	6.49	6.54	6.59	7.56	8.52	10.49	12.49
	.20	12	7.4	OBSERVATORY		8.16			10.16	10.21	11.16	12.57	1.02	2.46	3.46	3.51	4.46	5.46	6.46	6.51	6.56	7.53	8.49	10.46	12.46
5	.25	13	7.9	PROSPECT		8.14			10.14	10.19	11.14	12.56	1.01	2.44	3.44	3.49	4.44	5.44	6.44	6.49	6.54	7.52	8.47	10.44	12.44
	.25	14	8.9	HEALS		8.12			10.12	10.17	11.12	12.54	12.59	2.42	3.42	3.47	4.42	5.42	6.42	6.47	6.52	7.50	8.45	10.42	12.42
6	.30	15	9.7	RIFLE RANGE		8.10			10.10		11.10	12.52	12.57	2.40	3.40	3.45	4.40	5.40	6.40	6.45	6.50	7.48	8.43	10.40	12.40
	.30	16	10.2	DURRANCE		8.09			10.09		11.09	12.51	12.56	2.39	3.39	3.44	4.39	5.40	6.39	6.44	6.49	7.47	8.42	10.39	12.39
7	.35	17	11.2	TODD INLET		8.07			10.07		11.07	12.49	12.54	2.37	3.37	5.38	6.37	6.42	6.47	7.44	8.40	10.37	12.37		
	.35	18	11.6	BRENTWOOD		8.06			10.06		11.06	12.48	12.53	2.36	3.36	3.41	4.36	5.37	6.36	6.41	6.46	7.44	8.39	10.36	12.36
	.35	19	12.2	MARCHANT ROAD		8.04			10.04		11.04	12.46	12.51	2.34	3.34	3.39	4.34	5.35	6.34	6.39	6.44	7.42	8.36	10.32	12.32
	.35	20	12.5	SLUGGETTS		8.02			10.02		11.02	12.45	12.50	2.32	3.32	3.37	4.32	5.34	6.32	6.37	6.42	7.41	8.36	10.32	12.32
8	.40	21	13.6	STELLYS		7.59			9.59		10.59		12.48		3.29	3.34	4.29	5.31	6.29			7.38	8.33	10.29	12.29
	.40	22	14.2	PROSSER AVENUE		7.57			9.57	10.57		12.47		3.27	3.32	4.27	5.30	6.30			7.37	8.32	10.27	12.27	
	.40	22	14.9	SAANICHTON		7.55			9.55	10.55		12.45		3.25	3.30	4.25	5.28	6.25	6.30			7.35	8.30	10.25	12.25
9	.50	23	16.9	EXPERIMENTAL FARM				9.49			12.39		3.19			6.19							10.19		
	.50	24	17.4	BAZAN BAY				9.47			12.37		3.17			6.17							10.17		
	.50	25	17.8	TRIPP				9.45			12.36		3.15			6.15							10.15		
	.50	26	18.8	SIDNEWAY				9.42			12.33		3.12			6.12							10.12		
10	.60	27	19.4	MEADLANDS				9.40			12.32		3.10			6.10							10.10		
	.60	28	19.8	GIBSON'S CROSSING				9.38			12.30		3.08			6.08							10.08		
11	.65	29	20.9	MALLOWMOT				9.35			12.27		3.05			6.05							10.05		
	.65	30	22.3	TATLOW				9.30			12.23		3.00			6.00							10.00		
	.65	31	23.0	DEEP BAY				9.25			12.20		2.55			5.55							9.55		
					A.M.	A.M.	A.M.	A.M.	A.M.	A.M.	A.M.	A.M.	P.M.	P.M.	P.M.	P.M.	P.M.	P.M.	P.M.	P.M.	P.M.	P.M.	P.M.	P.M.	A.M.

Sunday service on the Saanich line
at the inauguration of one-man service
on May 27, 1923.

SUNDAYS. NORTHBOUND—Read Down

Zone Number	Fare From Victoria	Stat. Number	Miles From Victoria	STATIONS	A.M.	A.M.	A.M.	A.M.	P.M.	P.M.	P.M.	P.M.	P.M.	P.M.	P.M.	P.M.	P.M.	P.M.	P.M.	P.M.
1		1	.0	VICTORIA	7.30	9.30	10.30	11.30	1.30	1.35	3.30	4.30	5.30	5.35	6.30	7.30	8.30	8.35	9.00	10.30
	.05	2	1.9	HARRIETT	7.39	9.39	10.39	11.39	1.39	1.39	3.39	4.39	5.39	5.44	6.39	7.39	8.39	8.44	9.09	10.39
	.05	3	2.3	BURNSIDE RD. Way Pts.	7.40	9.40	10.40	11.40	1.40	1.45	3.40	4.40	5.40	5.45	6.40	7.40	8.40	8.45	9.10	10.40
2	.10	4	2.6	TILLICUM	7.43	9.43	10.43	11.43	1.43	1.48	3.43	4.43	5.43	5.48	6.43	7.43	8.43	8.48	9.13	10.43
	.10	5	3.4	MARIGOLD	7.46	9.46	10.46	11.46	1.46	1.51	3.46	4.46	5.46	5.51	6.46	7.46	8.46	8.51	9.16	10.46
3	.15	6	3.8	BLACKWOOD ROAD	7.48	9.48	10.48	11.48	1.48	1.53	3.48	4.48	5.48	5.53	6.48	7.48	8.48	8.53	9.18	10.48
	.15	7	4.3	WILKINSON	7.49	9.49	10.49	11.49	1.49	1.54	3.49	4.49	5.49	5.54	6.49	7.49	8.49	8.54	9.19	10.49
	.15	8	4.8	GLYN	7.51	9.51	10.51	11.51	1.51	1.56	3.51	4.51	5.51	5.56	6.51	7.51	8.51	8.56	9.21	10.51
	.15	9	5.4	EBERTS	7.54	9.54	10.54	11.54	1.54	1.59	3.54	4.54	5.54	5.59	6.54	7.54	8.54	8.59	9.24	10.54
4	.20	10	6.2	WESTWOODVALE	7.57	9.57	10.57	11.57	1.57	2.02	3.57	4.57	5.57	6.02		7.57	8.57	9.02	9.27	10.57
	.20	11	6.7	GOWARD	7.59	9.59	10.59	11.59	1.59	2.04	3.59	4.59	5.59	6.04		7.59	8.59	9.04	9.29	10.59
	.20	12	7.4	OBSERVATORY	8.01	10.01	11.01	12.01	2.01	2.06	4.01	5.01	6.01	6.06		8.01	9.01	9.06	9.31	11.01
5	.25	13	7.9	PROSPECT	8.02	10.02	11.02	12.02	2.02	2.07	4.02	5.02	6.02	6.07		8.04	9.02	9.07	9.32	11.02
	.25	14	8.9	HEALS	8.04	10.04	11.04	12.04	2.04	2.09	4.04	5.04	6.04	6.09		8.04	9.04	9.09	9.34	11.04
6	.30	15	9.7	RIFLE RANGE	8.07	10.07	11.07	12.07	2.07	2.12	4.07	5.07	6.07	6.12		8.07	9.07	9.12		11.07
	.30	16	10.2	DURRANCE	8.08	10.08	11.08	12.08	2.08	2.13	4.08	5.08	6.08	6.13		8.08	9.08	9.13		11.08
7	.35	17	11.2	TODD INLET	8.10	10.10	11.10	12.10	2.10	2.15	4.10	5.10	6.10	6.15		8.10	9.10	9.15		11.10
	.35	18	11.6	BRENTWOOD	8.11	10.11	11.11	12.11	2.11	2.16	4.11	5.11	6.11	6.16		8.11	9.11	9.16		11.11
	.35	19	12.2	MARCHANT ROAD	8.13	10.13	11.13	12.13	2.13	2.18	4.13	5.13	6.13	6.18		8.13	9.13	9.18		11.13
	.35	20	12.5	SLUGGETTS	8.14	10.14	11.14	12.14	2.14	2.19	4.14	5.14	6.14	6.19		8.14	9.14	9.19		11.14
8	.40	21	13.6	STELLYS	8.17	10.17	11.17	12.17	2.17	2.22	4.17	5.17	6.17			8.17	9.17			11.17
	.40	22	14.2	PROSSER AVENUE	8.18	10.18	11.18	12.18	2.18	2.23	4.18	5.18	6.18			8.18	9.18			11.18
	.40	22	14.9	SAANICHTON	8.20	10.20	11.20	12.20	2.20	2.25	4.20	5.20	6.20			8.20	9.20			11.20
9	.50	23	16.9	EXPERIMENTAL FARM	8.25		11.25		2.25				5.25			8.25				
	.50	24	17.4	BAZAN BAY	8.27		11.27		2.27				5.27			8.27				
	.50	25	17.8	TRIPP	8.28		11.28		2.28				5.28			8.28				
	.50	26	18.8	SIDNEWAY	8.31		11.31		2.31				5.31			8.31				
10	.60	27	19.4	MEADLANDS	8.33		11.33		2.33				5.33			8.33				
	.60	28	19.8	GIBSON'S CROSSING	8.35		11.35		2.35				5.35			8.35				
11	.65	29	20.9	MALLOWMOT	8.39		11.39		2.39				5.39			8.39				
	.65	30	22.3	TATLOW	8.43		11.43		2.43				5.43			8.43				
	.65	31	23.0	DEEP BAY	8.50		11.50		2.50				5.50			8.50				
					A.M.	A.M.	A.M.	A.M.	P.M.	P.M.	P.M.	P.M.	P.M.	P.M.	P.M.	P.M.	P.M.	P.M.	P.M.	P.M.

SUNDAYS. SOUTHBOUND—Read Up.

Zone Number	Fare From Victoria	Stat. Number	Miles From Victoria	STATIONS	A.M.	A.M.	P.M.	P.M.	P.M.	P.M.	P.M.	P.M.	P.M.	P.M.	P.M.	P.M.	P.M.	P.M.	P.M.	M.nday
1		1	.0	VICTORIA	10.20	11.20	1.20	1.25	2.25	4.20	5.20	7.20	7.25	7.30	7.35	10.20	10.25	10.30	10.35	12.20
	.05	2	1.9	HARRIETT	10.10	11.10	1.10	1.15	3.15	4.10	5.10	7.10	7.15	7.20	7.25	10.10	10.15	10.20	10.25	12.10
	.05	3	2.3	BURNSIDE RD. Way Pts.	10.06	11.06	1.06	1.11	3.11	4.06	5.06	7.06	7.11	7.16	7.21	10.06	10.11	10.16	10.21	12.06
2	.10	4	2.6	TILLICUM	10.05	11.05	1.05	1.10	3.10	4.05	5.05	7.05	7.10	7.15	7.20	10.05	10.10	10.15	10.20	12.05
	.10	5	3.4	MARIGOLD	10.02	11.02	1.02	1.07	3.07	4.02	5.02	7.02	7.07	7.12	7.17	10.02	10.07	10.12	10.17	12.02
3	.15	6	3.8	BLACKWOOD ROAD	10.00	11.00	1.00	1.05	3.05	4.00	5.00	7.00	7.05	7.10	7.15	10.00	10.05	10.10	10.15	12.00
	.15	7	4.3	WILKINSON	9.59	10.59	12.59	1.04	3.04	3.59	4.59	6.59	7.04	7.09	7.14	9.59	10.04	10.09	10.14	11.59
	.15	8	4.8	GLYN	9.57	10.57	12.57	1.02	3.02	3.57	4.57	6.57	7.02	7.07	7.12	9.57	10.02	10.07	10.12	11.57
	.15	9	5.4	EBERTS	9.54	10.54	12.54	12.59	2.59	3.54	4.54	6.54	6.59	7.04	7.09	9.54	9.59	10.04	10.09	11.54
4	.20	10	6.2	WESTWOODVALE	9.51	10.51	12.51	12.56	2.56	3.51	4.51	6.51	6.56	7.01		9.51	9.56	10.01	10.05	11.51
	.20	11	6.7	GOWARD	9.49	10.49	12.49	12.54	2.54	3.49	4.49	6.49	6.54	6.59		9.49	9.54	9.59	10.04	11.49
	.20	12	7.4	OBSERVATORY	9.46	10.46	12.46	12.51	2.51	3.46	4.46	6.46	6.51	6.56		9.46	9.51	9.56	10.01	11.46
5	.25	13	7.9	PROSPECT	9.44	10.44	12.44	12.49	2.49	3.44	4.44	6.44	6.49	6.54		9.44	9.49	9.54	9.59	11.44
	.25	14	8.9	HEALS	9.42	10.42	12.42	12.47	2.47	3.42	4.42	6.42	6.47	6.52		9.42	9.47	9.52	9.57	11.42
6	.30	15	9.7	RIFLE RANGE	9.40	10.40	12.40	12.45	2.45	3.40	4.40	6.40	6.45	6.50		9.40	9.45	9.50		11.40
	.30	16	10.2	DURRANCE	9.39	10.39	12.39	12.44	2.44	3.39	4.39	6.39	6.44	6.49		9.39	9.44	9.49		11.39
7	.35	17	11.2	TODD INLET	9.37	10.37	12.37	12.42	2.42	3.37	4.37	6.37	6.42	6.47		9.37	9.42	9.47		11.37
	.35	18	11.6	BRENTWOOD	9.36	10.36	12.36	12.41	2.41	3.36	4.36	6.36	6.41	6.46		9.36	9.41	9.46		11.36
	.35	19	12.2	MARCHANT ROAD	9.34	10.34	12.34	12.39	2.39	3.34	4.34	6.34	6.39	6.44		9.34	9.39	9.44		11.34
	.35	20	12.5	SLUGGETTS	9.32	10.32	12.32	12.37	2.37	3.32	4.32	6.32	6.37	6.42		9.32	9.37	9.42		11.32
8	.40	21	13.6	STELLYS	9.29	10.29	12.29	12.34	2.34	3.29	4.29	6.29	6.34			9.29	9.34			11.29
	.40	22	14.2	PROSSER AVENUE	9.27	10.27	12.27	12.32	2.32	3.27	4.27	6.27	6.32			9.27	9.32			11.27
	.40	22	14.9	SAANICHTON	9.25	10.25	12.25	12.30	2.30	3.25	4.25	6.25	6.30			9.25	9.30			11.25
9	.50	23	16.9	EXPERIMENTAL FARM	9.19		12.19		3.19			6.19				9.19				
	.50	24	17.4	BAZAN BAY	9.17		12.17		3.17			6.17				9.17				
	.50	25	17.8	TRIPP	9.15		12.15		3.15			6.15				9.15				
	.50	26	18.8	SIDNEWAY	9.12		12.12		3.12			6.12				9.12				
10	.60	27	19.4	MEADLANDS	9.10		12.10		3.10			6.10				9.10				
	.60	28	19.8	GIBSON'S CROSSING	9.08		12.08		3.08			6.08				9.08				
11	.65	29	20.9	MALLOWMOT	9.05		12.05		3.05			6.05				9.05				
	.65	30	22.3	TATLOW	9.00		12.00		3.00			6.00				9.00				
	.65	31	23.0	DEEP BAY	8.55		11.55		2.55			5.55				8.55				
					A.M.	A.M.	A.M.	P.M.	P.M.	P.M.	P.M.	P.M.	P.M.	P.M.	P.M.	P.M.	P.M.	P.M.	P.M.	P.M.

A ferry service connection with the Saanich line was attempted more than once, but to little effect. (Deep Cove is the older designation for Deep Bay.)

The Empress Hotel has replaced the backwaters
of James Bay, and a new esplanade,
or causeway, has supplanted James Bay Bridge
in this view north from the new parliament building.
RONALD A. GREENE COLLECTION

It's early morning on Dalhousie Street (Willows School looms
to the right) as a tardy tradesman begins to sprint for downtown-bound
Uplands car 253.   PABC

Cars 1706, 1240 and 1242 ▶
formed the special inaugural train
over the well-graded, splendidly-built
Saanich interurban line on June 18, 1913.
Most of the station shelters had
not yet received their coat of paint.
VICTORIA CITY ARCHIVES

In the 600-block of
Yates Street, looking east
to Douglas Street.
PABC

On June 18, 1913, at Deep Bay, the northern terminus
of the Saanich line, the Honourable Sir Richard
McBride, premier of British Columbia, drives
the last spike.   AUTHOR'S COLLECTION

The Saanich line's inaugural train
stops at Brentwood, on its return journey
to Victoria, to allow its guests
to inspect the Brentwood power plant.
H. R. HALLS PHOTO

An interior view of interurban car 1222,
similar to the Saanich line's 1239 - 1244 cars.
BOB WEBSTER PHOTO

Saanich line locomotive stalwart 98
finished out its lengthy career
on the Vancouver side of the Strait of Georgia
RONALD A. GREENE COLLECTION

A view from Pandora Avenue, just east of Douglas Street,
into the Saanich line's Victoria depot compound.
Notice the tracks turning off Pandora Avenue, to be cut off
by the fence. PABC

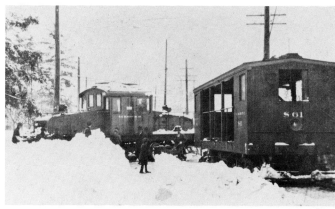

The great snow of 1916 took 981 off
the rails on the Saanich line,
bringing out wrecking car S.61.
GEOFF MEUGENS PHOTO

During the snows of February 1916,
the Saanich line's Victoria depot
compound, south from Cormorant Street.
Both buildings to the right
still adorn Pandora Avenue today.
TED CLARK PHOTO

The Saanich line, lonely under the snow of 1916.
GEOFF MEUGENS PHOTO

Car 386 ploughs through the snow of 1916, seemingly against traffic, past the Empress Hotel, out of sight to the right. PABC

Snow plow S.58, southbound, poses proudly in front of the city hall in February 1916. VICTORIA CITY ARCHIVES

Locomotive 906, at Esquimalt, performing its mission of mercy during the unusual snow of 1916, delivering coal to many households in difficulty. PABC

Saanich line locomotive 953 works south on Douglas Street in February 1916. The unfinished hulk of the Hudson's Bay Company's department store dominates the distant background. PABC

Brentwood Hotel, with B.C. Electric's
Brentwood power plant, to the left, in 1915. For a time,
the Saanch line operated special trains between
Victoria and the hotel. VICTORIA CITY ARCHIVES

The Saanich line's Tod Inlet station,
complete with refreshments booth,
posing traveller, and Velvet Ice Cream
inducement. GEOFF MEUGENS PHOTO

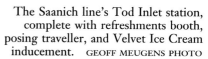

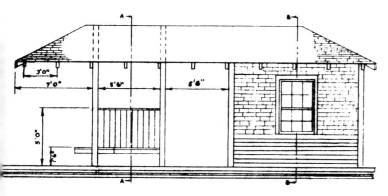

The Chalet at Deep Bay.
The photographer has taken the picture
from the platform of the
Saanich line's Deep Bay depot.
AUTHOR'S COLLECTION

Car 107 inaugurates the Foul Bay (Gonzales)
line on March 21, 1909. PABC

The engineer in his railway garb and the conductor in his
prepare for the twenty-three-mile run to Victoria
from the Saanich line's northern terminus, Deep Bay.
The walk to The Chalet leads to the left from the station.
TED CLARK PHOTO

The end of the Great War was cause for rejoicing and
celebration; appropriately, B.C. Electric's head office building
is adorned with flags, and Fort Street is packed
with Esquimalt's sailors. PABC

An Esquimalt-bound streetcar clatters over B.C. Electric's only
diamond crossing of another railway, the Esquimalt & Nanaimo,
on Esquimalt Road, near Springfield Street. PABC

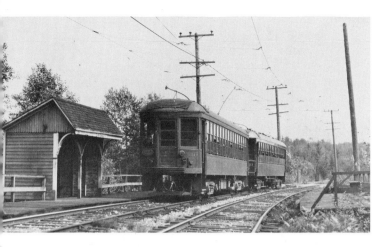

Former Saanich line coach 1240, together with 1221, at McGregor station on the heavily-travelled Central Park line connecting New Westminster and Vancouver. AUTHOR'S COLLECTION

Birney 405 at Pembroke Barn in 1922, showing Beacon Hill as its destination. TED CLARK PHOTO

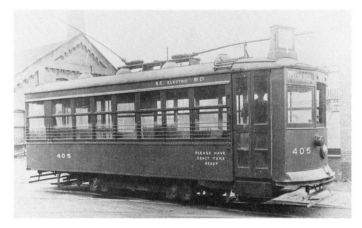

Car 381 in November 1921, the first Victoria streetcar equipped with "dead man" control. TED CLARK PHOTO

Car 22, splendidly rebuilt and ready to roll, on April 11, 1923; the inaugural trip of the Saanich line's brief one-man operation was a complete success. Operator Leonard Palmer is flanked by B.C. Electric officials and provincial railway inspector Rae. Rarely photographed passenger-mail car 1501 cools its heels to the left in the Victoria depot compound.
GEOFF MEUGENS PHOTO

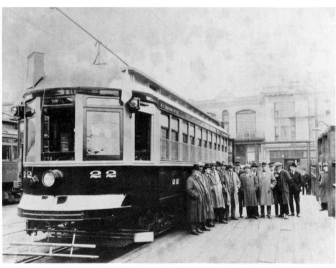

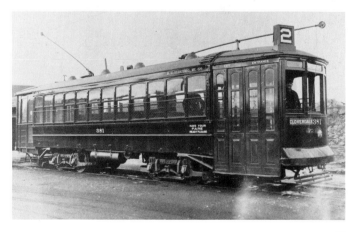

67

The Durrance family poses
before its depot namesake in 1923.
GEOFF MEUGENS PHOTO

One of three Saanich line trestles,
dominated by a flashy reminder
of why the interurban lasted
not even a dozen years.
GEOFF MEUGENS PHOTO

Tariff code posted on Prospect station
and new platform in place, rebuilt car 22
embarks passengers who, however,
may ride this spring 1923 journey
no farther than Saanichton.
"S" stood for Saanichton.
AUTHOR'S COLLECTION

Facing the late evening sun at Deep Bay,
operator G. Rhodes, with rebuilt car 23,
relaxes momentarily before "changing ends"
for the run back to Victoria.

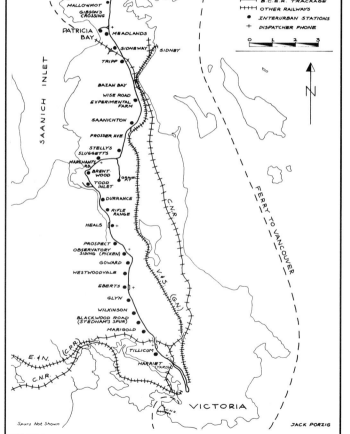

The Saanich line after track removal,
trolley hangers still in place.
GEOFF MEUGENS PHOTO

with sixteen feet of its length given to a car-width mail sorting and filing compartment.

Real trouble for the streetcars arrived on the scene towards the end of November: jitneys – named after the five-cent fare they charged – began following the same routes as the streetcars, picking up any willing riders. For many people, a ride into town in this fashion with two or three others was their very first ride in an automobile. If they did not break down, jitneys were faster than streetcars, and some jitney entrepreneurs went so far as to install benches, handle bars, and other appurtenances for the satisfaction of their frequently packed-in load of passengers. What began as a catch-as-catch-can, one-man operation quickly developed the clout to terrorize the most entrenched of streetcar systems, not excluding B.C. Electric. Approximately sixty jitneys were at work in greater Victoria by early 1915.

On January 11, 1915, Victoria General Motor Bus Company Limited began a half-hourly service between downtown and Willows.[37] B.C. Electric tried to compete by improving service, and on May 10, non-transfer streetcar tickets at eight for twenty-five cents (called "tango tickets") were introduced, but even this gambit did not reverse the trend and was abandoned on December 31.[38]

On Victoria's system, the following streetcars were available for service in 1915, although the small, original single truckers were stored at the Cloverdale barn, rarely, if ever, seeing city streets: 1 - 9, 11 - 13, 23, 27, 30, 69, 70, 123, 125, 126, 128, 183, 194, 231 - 240, 250 - 259 and 381 - 390. Other vehicles on the system included sprinkler car S.52, sweeper S.58, motorized flatcar S.60, motorized freight car S.61, dump car S.102, line car L.5 (ex-532), and locomotives 905 and 906. The Saanich line operated with interurban coaches 1239 - 1244, passenger-mail car 1501, baggage-express car 1706, and locomotives 953 and 981.

As an austerity measure, all vehicles lost some glamour when it came time for repainting, a straight green, minus the gold and white, now having to suffice. Even the sign boards had been simplified, now of one colour only, accompanied on the front of the car by a large matching sign with a large number, designating the car's route.

When Tuesday, February 1, 1916 dawned, nine inches of snow had fallen overnight, just the beginning of the Victoria area's greatest snowfall ever. The transmission line from Jordan River was down, and 130 men of the 88th Fusiliers were attempting to find the rails of the Mt. Tolmie streetcar line. Three gangs of several hundred men had enabled the Saanich line to resume full service on February 10. Locomotive 906, with flatcars, delivered tons of coal to Victoria's extremities, Esquimalt and Oak Bay. B.C. Electric granted the five hundred soldiers who had worked on snow removal for the streetcar and interurban lines free rides across the greater Victoria system from February 20 to March 20. Jitneys were soon out again, but their number was down because of tire wear and a rise in the price of gasoline.

In June, in an attractive public relations move, the company instituted a weekly informational leaflet which would soon be titled *The Buzzer*. The Victoria-based and Vancouver-based systems each produced their own version, replete with company notes, schedules, community information, helpful hints, and jokes and anecdotes. (B.C. Electric's successor, B.C. Transit, still produces the two versions today, still headed by the same title.)

On November 1, B.C. Electric introduced the staff system of signalling on single track, or at places where double tracks converged into single track. Two of the lines, Foul Bay and Uplands, actually used three different staffs; in the case of Foul Bay, a yellow one was employed between Foul Bay terminus and the siding at Arnold Avenue, a red one between Arnold and Joseph streets, and a green one between the latter and the corner of Cook Street and Fairfield Road. All staffs were exchanged at the points named on each staff or, if the opposite car had not reached the point, at the first point it was met after passing such a point on double track. Gorge and Foul Bay were the only exceptions, the staff being locked in a box on a convenient pole.[39]

Near the end of February 1917, B.C. Electric for the first time issued school children's certificates, to be issued by school principals in Victoria, Esquimalt and Oak Bay to cut down on the wide-spread abuse of the low rate of fare granted to school children.

With all the road building and resurfacing occurring in Saanich, the heavy losses being incurred by the V. & S., and the reluctance of shippers to indulge in the formalities of using the Saanich line, astonishingly, a third Saanich railway, Canadian Northern Pacific's (later Canadian National's), went into service on April 30, from Victoria, sixteen miles to a ferry slip at Patricia Bay. As the V. & S., it used a gas-electric motor car giving twice-daily service, except on Sundays. B.C. Electric's line interchanged with the new line only at Tripp.

Realizing that the V. & S. had very little time left, B.C. Electric officials began planning for salvaging the best features of the V. & S. The first priority was entry into Sidney, and to that end, the "Bazan Bay Tie Line" was surveyed and mapped; it angled off to the north from the Saanich line at a point today occupied by the northeast corner of the Sansbury Elementary school grounds, and connected with the V. & S. just before its crossover with the C.N.P. The other

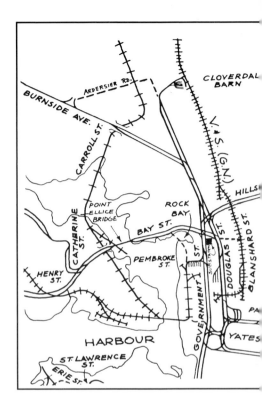

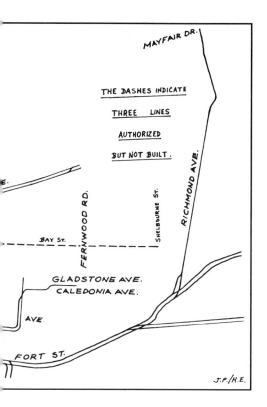

THE DASHES INDICATE
THREE LINES
AUTHORIZED
BUT NOT BUILT.

J.P./H.E.

priority was to take over the Victoria terminal facilities of the V. & S. on Blanshard Street between Fisgard and Pembroke streets, and to that end, B.C. Electric designed an 800-foot, single-track line on Bay Street, connecting the streetcar line on Douglas Street with the V. & S. main line to the east, calling it the "Bay Street Tie Link." However, though the arrival of the C.N.P. had created further havoc, by the time the V. & S. would give up the ghost (it would send its gas-electric coach to the U.S. mainland in September and cut back to one steam locomotive-drawn passenger train per day, and two freights per week), B.C. Electric would have lost interest in it.

The death of Victoria's streetcar founder, D. W. Higgins in 1917 had sounded a sombre note in a difficult time. The inauguration of a truck service between Victoria and Sidney in October was another kind of bad news, but the opening of the Dominion Observatory along the Saanich line on May 6, 1918 was an obvious boon; its telescope, at 72 inches, was the largest in the world. In anticipation of the event, B.C. Electric had renamed Picken station "Observatory," and the company lost not a beat in promoting travel by interurban train to the new facility.

On August 12, street railway men achieved an eight-hour work day, the same day the first electric switch on the Victoria streetcar system became operative, at busy Oak Bay Junction, Fort Street at Oak Bay Avenue. Double-tracked Fort Street, west from the junction to Yates Street, had been known locally for some three years now as "the Dardanelles" – named after the Great War battles in early 1915 – because of its constricted roadway, hardly allowing passage for even one motor car if a streetcar was in progress.

In early 1919, the C.N.P. abandoned its Saanich passenger service, and on April 30, the V. & S. operated its last passenger train;

its last train movement, a freight, passed over the quarter-century-old railway on May 8.[40] B.C. Electric's line now had Saanich to itself.

With the linkage of the Mt. Tolmie and Burnside lines on March 24, "No. 8, Burnside" disappeared completely, Victoria's streetcar numbering possessing the following configuration:

 1 Oak Bay
 2 Outer Wharf–Cloverdale
 3 Beacon Hill–Fernwood
 4 Esquimalt
 5 Gorge
 6 Foul Bay
 7 Hillside
 9 Uplands
10 Mt. Tolmie–Burnside
11 Willows

Because it had seen very little use in Victoria, observation streetcar 123 was sent to Vancouver in April, where it joined its twin 124 for thirty-two more summers of sightseeing.

New bylaws were passed on December 1, 1920 in Victoria, Esquimalt and Oak Bay prohibiting jitney operators from competing with streetcars on their routes and applying a variety of rules and regulations to jitney operators. Although the jitney phase was thereby done with, it escaped no one's attention that rubber-tired, trackless transportation had a future. Along with the jitney settlement came a raised fare, six cents, or six tickets for 35 cents.

On December 22, the No. 6 and No. 7 lines were linked to form a new line, numbered 6, through routed via Douglas, Fort, Cook and May streets, omitting the Government Street-included loop-around. Those streetcars operating the Foul Bay end only to Arnold (in later years Joseph Street) would be the only ones to display a number 7, although initially they sported only a distinctive sign.

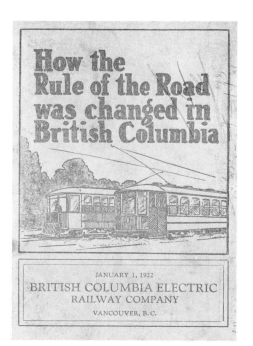

How the Rule of the Road was changed in British Columbia

JANUARY 1, 1922
BRITISH COLUMBIA ELECTRIC
RAILWAY COMPANY
VANCOUVER, B.C.

With the institution of right-hand drive announced by the provincial government for January 1, 1922, 1921 was a year of preparation for B.C. Electric. Besides the rebuilding of the streetcars, the company would have to contend with reversing its numerous track crossovers and electric switches, as well as their attendant trolley wires. The changes to the cars themselves had to be boarded up and kept in an inoperable condition until New Year's Day. Some cars, the 250s, were simply turned about, with their long Detroit-platformed rear vestibule becoming the front, motorman's vestibule.

What better time for the company to announce that its streetcars would become one-man operated! Not only employees but also many municipal officials opposed this move. Soon after this announcement on September 21, 1921, the company ordered ten single-truck, "safety cars," known as Birneys, after their creator, Charles O. Birney, the engineer responsible for steet car design and construction for U.S. transit giant, the Stone & Webster Corporation. Short and light – one-third of the weight of conventional streetcars – and safe, because of their "dead man" control, these cars offered economy and reliability, and they would come to Victoria equipped for right-hand operation. (Since the Birneys had been introduced in 1916, more than 4,000 had been placed in service.)

The "dead man" control combined in one handle the brake, emergency valve, door opener and sander. The first Victoria streetcar equipped with this control was car 381 which put in a successful shift on the Gorge line on November 11, followed by work on the Mt. Tolmie run. All Victoria streetcars would shortly be similarly equipped.

At the height of the right-hand and one-man excitement, the new Cleveland Fare Box, mounted in permanent position, came

75

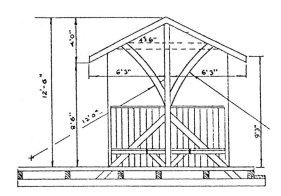

The "outdoor" end of the typical
Saanich line station.

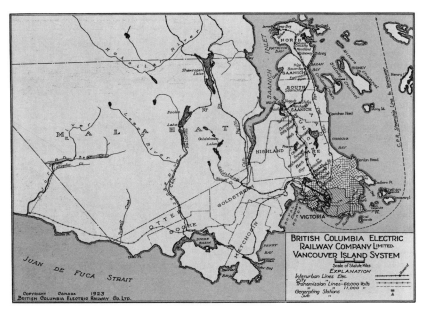

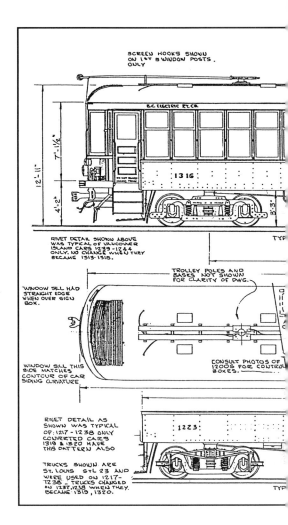

B.C. Electric territory in 1923, at the southern extremity
of Vancouver Island. Notice Jordan River
at far left, as well as the Saanich interurban line,
still in place for one last year. AUTHOR'S COLLECTION

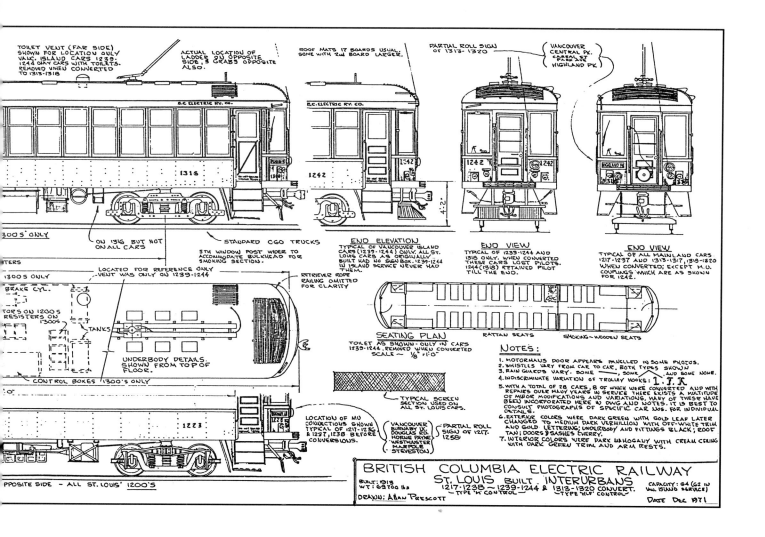

TOILET VENT (FAR SIDE) SHOWN FOR LOCATION ONLY. VANC. ISLAND CARS 1239-1244 ONLY CARS WITH TOILETS. REMOVED WHEN CONVERTED TO 1313-1318.

ACTUAL LOCATION OF LADDER ON OPPOSITE SIDE, 3 GRABS OPPOSITE ALSO.

ROOF MATS 17 BOARDS USUAL. SOME WITH 2ND BOARD LARGER.

PARTIAL ROLL SIGN OF 1313-1320

VANCOUVER CENTRAL PK. CAREALL 57 HIGHLAND PK

B.C. ELECTRIC RY. CO.

1318

1300

B.C. ELECTRIC RY. CO.

1242

1242   1242

HIGHLAND PK
1315

1300'S ONLY

ON 1316 BUT NOT ON ALL CARS

STANDARD C60 TRUCKS

5TH WINDOW POST WIDER TO ACCOMMODATE BULKHEAD FOR SMOKING SECTION.

END ELEVATION
TYPICAL OF VANCOUVER ISLAND CARS (1239-1244) ONLY. ALL ST. LOUIS CARS AS ORIGINALLY BUILT HAD NO SIGN BOX. 1239-1244 IN ISLAND SERVICE NEVER HAD THEM.

END VIEW
TYPICAL OF 1239-1244 AND 1318 ONLY. WHEN CONVERTED THESE CARS LOST PILOTS. 1244 (1318) RETAINED PILOT TILL THE END.

END VIEW
TYPICAL OF ALL MAINLAND CARS 1217-1237 AND 1313-1317, 1319-1320 WHEN CONVERTED; EXCEPT M.U. COUPLINGS WHICH ARE AS SHOWN FOR 1242.

1300'S ONLY

TERS

BRAKE CYL.

TORS ON 1200'S RESISTERS ON 1300'S

TANKS

LOCATED FOR REFERENCE ONLY - VENT WAS ONLY ON 1239-1244

RETRIEVER ROPE RAILING OMITTED FOR CLARITY

UNDERBODY DETAILS SHOWN FROM TOP OF FLOOR.

CONTROL BOXES 1300'S ONLY

SEATING PLAN
TOILET AS SHOWN - ONLY IN CARS 1239-1244. REMOVED WHEN CONVERTED
SCALE ~ 1/8" 1'-0"

RATTAN SEATS

SMOKING~WOODEN SEATS

TYPICAL SCREEN SECTION USED ON ALL ST. LOUIS CARS.

NOTES:
1. MOTORMANS DOOR APPEARS PANELLED IN SOME PHOTOS.
2. WHISTLES VARY FROM CAR TO CAR, BOTH TYPES SHOWN
3. RAIN GUARDS VARY. SOME ——, ——, AND SOME NONE.
4. INDISCRIMINATE VARIATION OF TROLLEY HOOKS: ⌐ ⌐ ⌐
5. WITH A TOTAL OF 28 CARS, 8 OF WHICH WERE CONVERTED AND WITH REPAIRS OVER MANY YEARS IN SERVICE THERE EXISTS A MULTITUDE OF MINOR MODIFICATIONS AND VARIATIONS. MANY OF THESE HAVE (BEEN) INCORPORATED HERE IN DWG AND NOTES. IT IS BEST TO CONSULT PHOTOGRAPHS OF SPECIFIC CAR NOS. FOR INDIVIDUAL DETAILS.
6. EXTERIOR COLORS WERE DARK GREEN WITH GOLD LEAF LATER CHANGED TO MEDIUM DARK VERMILLION WITH OFF-WHITE TRIM AND GOLD LETTERING; UNDERBODY AND FITTINGS BLACK; ROOF TAN; DOORS & SASHES CHERRY.
7. INTERIOR COLORS WERE DARK MAHOGANY WITH CREAM CEILING WITH DARK GREEN TRIM AND ARM RESTS.

1223

1223

LOCATION OF MU CONNECTIONS SHOWN TYPICAL OF 1217-1236 & 1237,1238 BEFORE CONVERSIONS.

VANCOUVER BURNABY LK. DOUGLAS RD. HORNE PAYNE WESTMINSTER MARPOLE STEVESTON

PARTIAL ROLL SIGN OF 1217-1258

OPPOSITE SIDE - ALL ST. LOUIS' 1200'S

BRITISH COLUMBIA ELECTRIC RAILWAY
ST. LOUIS BUILT INTERURBANS
1217-1238 ~ 1239-1244 & 1313-1320 CONVERT.
—TYPE "H" CONTROL—   —TYPE "HLF" CONTROL—

BUILT: 1913
WT: 69,700 lbs
DRAWN: Allan Prescott

CAPACITY: 64 (62 IN VAN. ISLAND SERVICE)

DATE DEC 1971

BRITISH COLUMBIA ELECTRIC RAILWAY COMPANY, LIMITED

LOCAL PASSENGER TARIFF
BETWEEN POINTS ON THE
SAANICH DIVISION
AS SHOWN HEREIN

Miles from Victoria	Zone No.	Station No.	STATIONS	Fares
.0	1	1	Victoria	0
1.9	1	2	Harriett Road	5
2.3	1	3	Burnside Road Way Points	5 5
2.6	2	4	Tillicum	10 5 5
3.4	2	5	Marigold	10 5 5 5
3.8	3	6	Blackwood Road	15 15 10 10 5
4.3	3	7	Wilkinson	15 15 10 10 5 5
4.8	3	8	Glyn	15 15 10 10 5 5 5
5.4	3	9	Eberts	15 15 10 10 5 5 5 5
6.2	4	10	Westwoodvale	20 20 15 15 10 10 10 5 5
6.7	4	11	Goward	20 20 15 15 10 10 10 5 5 5
7.4	4	12	Observatory	20 20 15 15 10 10 10 5 5 5 5
7.9	5	13	Prospect	25 25 20 20 20 15 15 15 10 10 10 5
8.9	5	14	Heals	25 25 20 20 20 15 15 15 10 10 10 5 5
9.7	6	15	Rifle Range	30 30 25 20 20 20 15 15 15 10 10 5 5 5
10.2	6	16	Durrance	30 30 25 20 20 20 15 15 15 10 10 5 5 5 5
11.2	7	17	Tod Inlet	35 35 30 25 25 25 20 20 20 15 15 15 10 10 5 5
11.6	7	18	Brentwood	35 35 30 25 25 25 20 20 20 15 15 15 10 10 5 5 5
12.2	7	19	Marchant Road	35 35 30 25 25 25 20 20 20 15 15 15 10 10 5 5 5 5
12.5	7	20	Sluggetts	35 35 30 25 25 25 20 20 20 15 15 15 10 10 5 5 5 5 5
13.6	8	21	Stellys	40 40 35 35 35 35 30 30 30 25 25 25 20 20 15 15 10 10 10 5
14.9	8	22	Saanichton	40 40 35 35 35 35 30 30 30 25 25 25 20 20 15 15 10 10 10 5 5
16.9	9	23	Experimntl Farm or Wise Road	50 50 45 40 40 40 40 40 35 35 35 30 30 25 25 25 20 15 15 10 5
17.4	9	24	Bazan Bay	50 50 45 40 40 40 40 40 35 35 35 30 30 25 25 25 20 15 15 10 5 5
17.8	9	25	Tripp	50 50 45 40 40 40 40 40 35 35 35 30 30 25 25 25 20 15 15 10 5 5 5
18.8	9	26	Sidneway	50 50 45 40 40 40 40 40 35 35 35 30 30 25 25 25 20 15 15 10 5 5 5 5
19.4	10	27	Meadlands	60 60 55 55 50 50 45 45 40 40 40 35 35 35 30 30 25 25 20 20 15 15 10 10 10 5
19.8	10	28	Gibson's Crossing	60 60 55 55 50 50 45 45 40 40 40 35 35 35 30 30 25 25 20 20 15 15 10 10 10 5 5
20.9	11	29	Mallowmot	65 65 60 55 50 50 50 50 45 45 45 40 40 40 35 35 30 30 25 20 15 15 15 10 10 5
22.3	11	30	Tatlow	65 65 60 55 50 50 50 50 45 45 45 40 40 40 35 35 30 30 25 20 15 15 15 10 10 5 5
23.0	11	31	Deep Bay	65 65 60 55 50 50 50 50 45 45 45 40 40 40 35 35 30 30 25 20 20 15 15 15 10 10 5 5 5 0

Column stations (bottom header): Victoria, Harriett Road, Burnside Road Way Points, Tillicum, Marigold, Blackwood Road, Wilkinson, Glyn, Eberts, Westwoodvale, Goward, Observatory, Prospect, Heals, Rifle Range, Durrance, Tod Inlet, Brentwood, Marchant Road, Sluggetts, Stellys, Saanichton, Experimental Farm or Wise Rd., Bazan Bay, Tripp, Sidneway, Meadlands, Gibson's Crossing, Mallowmot, Tatlow, Deep Bay

RULE 1—Figures indicate the cost of Single-Journey Tickets.

RULE 2—Tickets in sheets (10 tickets to each sheet) will be issued for the benefit of Residents and Settlers at the rate of 75 cents for 20 Tickets. Minimum quantity sold: $3.00 for 8 sheets, or 80 Tickets.

RULE 3—Children five years of age and under twelve years will be carried at half the rates quoted in the above Tariff, except that no One-Way Fare shall be less than 5 cents.
Where Half Fare ends in figures other than 0 or 5, add 2½ cents to make fare end in 0 or 5.

RULE 4—School Children's Tickets will be issued in sheets (20 tickets to each sheet) at the rate of 55 cents per sheet.

RULE 5—Children under 5 years of age will be carried free only when accompanied by parents or guardians.

Issued March, 1923
Effective April, 1923

B. C. E. R. No. 23
CANCELLING B. C. E. R. No. 22

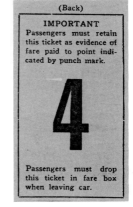

Saanich line passenger tariff and ticket at the inauguration of one-man service, May 27, 1923.
AUTHOR'S COLLECTION

SPECIAL SUNDAY SCHEDULE
SAANICH INTERURBAN
(ABRIDGED TIME TABLE)
EFFECTIVE ON AND AFTER SUNDAY, MAY 11, AND UNTIL FURTHER NOTICE

	A.M.	A.M.	A.M.	A.M.	P.M.	P.M.	P.M.	P.M.	P.M.	P.M.	P.M.	P.M.	P.M.	P.M.	P.M.
VICTORIA (Lve.)	7.30	9.30	10.30	11.30	1.30	1.35	3.30	4.30	5.30	5.35	7.30	8.30	8.35	9.00	10.30
WILKINSON	7.49	9.49	10.49	11.49	1.49	1.54	3.49	4.49	5.49	5.54	7.49	8.49	8.54	9.19	10.49
PROSPECT	8.02	10.02	11.02	12.02	2.02	2.07	4.02	5.02	6.02	6.07	8.02	9.02	9.07	9.32	11.02
TOD INLET (Butchart's Gardens)	8.10	10.10	11.10	12.10	2.10	2.15	4.10	5.10	6.10	6.15	8.10	9.10	9.15	......	11.10
BRENTWOOD	8.11	10.11	11.11	12.11	2.11	2.16	4.11	5.11	6.11	6.16	8.11	9.11	9.16	......	11.11
SAANICHTON	8.20	10.20	11.20	12.20	2.20	2.25	4.20	5.20	6.20	......	8.20	9.20	......	......	11.20
EXPERIMENTAL	8.25	......	11.25	......	2.25	......	......	5.25	......	......	8.25	......	......	......	......
DEEP BAY (Arr.)	8.50	......	11.50	......	2.50	......	......	5.50	......	......	8.50	......	......	......	......

	A.M.	A.M.	A.M.	P.M.	P.M.	P.M.	P.M.	P.M.	P.M.	P.M.	P.M.	P.M.	P.M.	P.M.	P.M.
DEEP BAY (Lve.)	8.55	......	11.55	......	......	2.55	......	5.55	......	......	8.55	......	......	......	......
EXPERIMENTAL	9.19	......	12.19	......	......	3.19	......	6.19	......	......	9.19	......	......	......	......
SAANICHTON	9.25	10.25	12.25	12.30	2.30	3.25	4.25	6.25	6.30	......	9.25	9.30	......	......	11.25
BRENTWOOD	9.36	10.36	12.36	12.41	2.41	3.36	4.36	6.36	6.41	6.46	9.36	9.41	9.46	......	11.36
TOD INLET (Butchart's Gardens)	9.37	10.37	12.37	12.42	2.42	3.37	4.37	6.37	6.42	6.47	9.37	9.42	9.47	......	11.37
PROSPECT	9.44	10.44	12.44	12.49	2.49	3.44	4.44	6.44	6.49	6.54	9.44	9.49	9.54	9.59	11.44
WILKINSON	9.59	10.59	12.59	1.04	3.04	3.59	4.59	6.59	7.04	7.09	9.59	10.04	10.09	10.14	11.59
VICTORIA (Arr.)	10.20	11.20	1.20	1.25	3.25	4.20	5.20	7.20	7.25	7.30	10.20	10.25	10.30	10.35	12.20 A.M.

into use on all streetcars; here was a convenient and stable fare-receiving device, especially well suited to one-man operation, to replace the hand-held Coleman "jugs" or "coffee pots."

One-man streetcar service got underway on February 13, 1922 with two cars on the Mt. Tolmie–Burnside route, and by April 16, the whole system was one-man operated. The ten double-ended Birneys, from Preston Car and Coach Company, which had been assembled at B.C. Electric's Kitsilano shops in Vancouver had been quickly put in service on the No. 2 line. Though very compact, they had a seating capacity of 32, and enough room for twenty standees. They were soon shared with the No. 3 line.

When in August residents in south Oak Bay and east of the terminal loop of the Foul Bay line petitioned for a streetcar line to connect the Foul Bay and Oak Bay termini, company official G. M. Tripp, who had recently studied trackless trolley (trolley coach) operations in the eastern U.S., replied that a streetcar line over the numerous grades and curves on such a proposed route would be prohibitively expensive, but that a trackless trolley given a solid road base could be a better solution.

Since Saanich municipality was still tolerating jitneys, B.C. Electric grasped at a possible solution, in October developing plans and specifications for five one-man streetcars for the Saanich line, 22, 23, 231, 232 and 233, to replace the large interurban cars. If the line were to survive, it would require all the coddling possible.

Remembered today by many British Columbians by the mountain lake near Vancouver named after him, Johannes Buntzen, one of the true builders of the province, died on October 2 in Copenhagen, Denmark. B.C. Electric's very existence had depended not only on his organizational and executive talents but also on

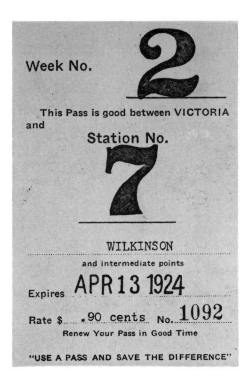

Week No. 2

This Pass is good between VICTORIA and

Station No. 7

WILKINSON

and intermediate points

Expires APR 13 1924

Rate $ .90 cents No. 1092

Renew Your Pass in Good Time

"USE A PASS AND SAVE THE DIFFERENCE"

his generosity and his intensity in every aspect of the company's activities.

One-man, PAYE (with the Cleveland Fare Box) service went into effect on the Saanich line on Sunday, May 27, 1923, with cars 22 and 23, extensively rebuilt, replacing interurban coaches 1239 - 1244 (and 1706), shipped to Vancouver. (Car 1501 would stay.) Cars 231 - 233 had been somewhat reworked and were available for Saanich line use, although the occasions would be rare; even car 234 had acquired train flag brackets at each end. In addition to five weekday round trips to Deep Bay, a generous schedule of runs to Saanichton, Sluggetts, Heals, and Eberts was set out in "Saanich Division Time Table No. 11." On Sundays, sixteen trains left Victoria, five all the way to Deep Bay (one way, 65 cents).

After February's snowfalls of almost 1916's proportions, for the coming winter, a mate for Victoria's lone snow sweeper S.58, S.59, arrived in time for the coming winter.

After years of controversy – B.C. Electric had long ago withdrawn from the planning committee – Johnson Street Bridge was opened on January 11, 1924.[41] Actually two separate spans in one, the northern span carried the E. & N., and the wider southern one, with streetcar tracks laid, but never used, carried two lanes of automobiles.

Although an unbelievably inexpensive pass system was tried on the Saanich line, even to granting free admissions to the Capitol, Dominion, and Royal Victoria theatres on certain days, ridership did not grow. B.C. Electric even sold The Chalet at Deep Bay (which had never become the hotel the company had intended).

From the Saanich line's inception until June 30, 1924, 3,096,541 passengers had been carried, for a loss in operations, excluding any interest on the investment, of $262, 299.10. As the September issue of *The Buzzer* stated, "In view of all the circumstances, it is not only very poor business policy but quite impossible to continue operation, and there can be little doubt that, while the line may at one time have been a necessity, it is so no longer – especially when the number of buses and stages operating is taken in consideration."

Friday, October 31 was the Saanich line's final day of operation. Passenger-mail coach 1501, having worked on the dismantling of the line, would not be returned to Vancouver until April 1928, but streetcars 22, 23 and 231-233 returned to full-time streetcar work in Victoria, with 22 and 23 appropriately assigned to the Mt. Tolmie-Burnside run, Burnside Road having been, of course, the exit route to Deep Bay. Upon the termination of interurban service, the western terminus of Burnside service had been cut back three blocks to Carroll Street. Fourteen miles of the interurban's right of way became part of Saanich municipality's road network.

In spring of 1925, Victoria was in an extraordinary tizzy as its ice hockey Cougars vanquished the vaunted Montreal Canadiens to win the Stanley Cup, three games to one. All the games in the series except one (staged for massive gate receipts in the larger arena in Vancouver) were played at the arena at the Willows,[42] across the street from today's Oak Bay Senior Secondary School. Even extra streetcars had been taxed to their limits.

B.C. Electric's deep-green paint scheme on its streetcars and interurban coaches had always been seriously attractive, especially with gold highlighting, but the new brilliance of Vancouver's ten sets of multiple-unit streetcars arriving from Canadian Car and Foundry Company in Montreal in their carmine-red with cream trim was almost frivolously explosive. Green was gone, and on November 30, the first repainted streetcar anywhere on the company's system appeared, to dazzle Oak Bay riders. Furthermore, by

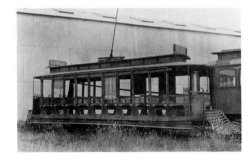

Car 11 in 1926, showing "Gorge," but unused for years, at Cloverdale barn. Car 28 to the right. B.C. HYDRO PHOTO

The interior of car 29 in 1926.
B.C. HYDRO PHOTO

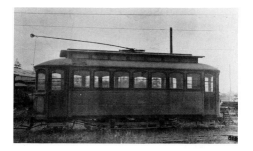

Car 29 in 1926, languishing at Cloverdale
barn. B.C. HYDRO PHOTO

the beginning of 1926, tungsten lamps were replacing the obsolete carbon filament globes on the streetcars.

Thirty-one years as a British company ended for B.C. Electric with the incorporation on May 19, 1928 of the British Columbia Power Corporation Limited, which had purchased the preferred and deferred ordinary shares of B.C. Electric.[43] Eastern Canadian investors, led by principal directors Herbert Holt and A. J. Nesbitt, were the successors to Robert Horne-Payne and his colleagues, although the B.C. Electric name would remain, as would its management.

Chairman of B.C. Electric since 1897, Horne-Payne, an invalid because of a recent stroke at his Brentwood home near London, retired in September. His visionary action on behalf of B.C. Electric had given massive input to creating British Columbia, as much by the infusion of his personal fortune as by his executive genius. Horne-Payne would die within a few months, on January 30, 1929.

On the last day of 1928, George Kidd retired as president of B.C. Electric (his title had been changed from general manager in 1923), to be succeeded by William George Murrin. This was also the year in which a serious competitor for the company, Vancouver Island Coach Lines, was formed. In September 1929, Royal Blue Line Motor Tours inaugurated an Oak Bay run, moving its operations off Fort Street and onto Yates Street only after the city's solicitor agreed with B.C. Electric's reminder that jitneys must not follow streetcar lines.

Because the Royal Blue Line initiated another line, Haultain, B.C. Electric finally retaliated by creating its own Haultain bus service, its first Victoria bus line, in December. An era had ended on November 10 with the spectacular destruction by fire of the ice arena, and so had another, although no one was quite sure of the implications at the time. Panic had begun in late October at New York's stock exchange, and on October 29, it experienced the heaviest day's trading in its history; even the best stocks were in tatters and investors lost their life's savings. A ten-year depression had begun and its effects would be felt soon enough.

B.C. Electric's new art-deco Bay Street substation, at the southeast corner of Bay and Government streets went into full service in March 1930. At this time Victoria's complement of forty-nine streetcars consisted of cars 22, 23, 125, 126, 128, 188, 189, 192, 194, 231 - 240, 250 - 259, 381 - 390 and 400 - 409, all wooden cars except for the 400-numbered Birneys. Locomotives 905 and 906, line car L.5, sprinkler and (now) rail grinder car S.52, snow sweepers S.58 and S.59, and wrecking car/"auxiliary service car" S.61 completed the roster, aside from the Hicks maintenance of way flatcar, 6111, the Simplex steel dump car, 0286, and the Hayes-Anderson tower truck, purchased during the year.

With falling patronage in Victoria, cars 125, 126 and 194 were barged to Vancouver, cars 128, 192 and 251 following in March 1931. Although 1934 was the nadir of ridership in greater Victoria – 6,053,441 passengers on the streetcars and 387,122 on the three Haultain buses – Foul Bay at least received some relief with the changing of its streetcar destination sign to "Gonzales" on December 27.

On April 11, 1936, British Columbians sustained the loss of one of the most esteemed builders of the province, Sir Frank Stillman Barnard, who died on that date at his Esquimalt foreshore family home, "Clovelly," on Barnard Avenue. It was Barnard who had attracted English money on which to base B.C.'s three little west coast streetcar systems; in addition, he served as member of parliament, and later as the province's lieutenant-governor.

THE BUZZER

Published by the British Columbia Electric Railway Co.

Vol. 8   VICTORIA, MONDAY, APRIL 28th, 1924   No. 48

Seeing Victoria and District by Trolley Car

B. C. ELECTRIC CITY CARS

Route Number
and Name

1. **OAK BAY**—Leaving the city loop via Government Street (south), proceeding through the residential district of Fort Street to Oak Bay Junction, turning down Oak Bay Avenue and through the Oak Bay residential district to the terminus at Oak Bay. There is an excellent hotel at this point, some particularly charming scenery of sea and distant mountains. Boats and launches are obtainable at the Oak Bay boathouse, which is a short distance from the car terminus. Cars leave on the hour and every 7½ minutes.

2. **OUTER WHARF**—Leaving the city loop via Government Street (south), passing the General Post Office, Empress Hotel, Inner Harbour (C.P.R. Wharves), Provincial Government Buildings, proceeding along Superior Street to the Outer Wharves, at which point the Transpacific and California boats dock. Cars leave the city on the hour and every 10 minutes.

3. **BEACON HILL**—Leaving the city loop via Government Street (south), passing the General Post Office, Empress Hotel, Inner Harbour (C.P.R. Wharves), Provincial Government Buildings, along Superior Street, Menzies Street and Niagara Street to the terminus at Beacon Hill Park.

MAKE A NOTE

To Renew Your Weekly Pass in Good Time.

Use It Frequently and Allow Other Members of Your Family to Use It.

B.C. Electric

COURTEOUS, EFFICIENT SERVICE

VANCOUVER   VICTORIA   NEW WESTMINSTER

Published by the British Columbia Electric Railway Co.

Vol. 17	VICTORIA, MONDAY, OCTOBER 3, 1932	No. 18

Busting the Depression
It's a Cinch With a Weekly Pass

COMING down town on the 8.05 a few mornings ago, we took our accustomed place at the back of the car and watched the rest of the 8.05 gang assemble as the car travelled towards the town. Each member of the gang was given an appropriate greeting as he arrived.

"Where's old G——, this morning?" asked someone. "He usually gets on about here." "Bet you a dollar he has slept in and missed his car," said someone else. "My gosh, here

Extremely worrisome for the company was the net loss in 1936 to Victoria's streetcar and bus system of $77,375.90, the highest in its history. Two more streetcars, 382 and 385, were sent to Vancouver in August 1937, car 386 in December, and car 384 early in 1937.

During the Royal visit in May 1939 a B.C.E.R. "Birney" was dressed up and travelled along Government Street. This 16 mm film frame captures it in front of the Belmont Building. MONTE WRIGHT PHOTO

CHAPTER III

B.C. Electric's Half Century: *The Final Decade – Triumph and Demise*

B.C. Electric Railway Co. Ltd.

03817

ESQUIMALT

A M	P M	HOUR
1		15 30 45
2		15 30 45
3		15 30 45
4		15 30 45
5		15 30 45
6		15 30 45
7		15 30 45
8		15 30 45
9		15 30 45
10		15 30 45
11		15 30 45
12		15 30 45

CONDITIONS—This transfer does not permit a stop-over and is not transferable, and will not be accepted unless presented on date of issue and before expiry of the time limit punched thereon, nor unless presented at a point where the line to which the transfer is given leaves the line on which the transfer is issued. Mutilated transfers not accepted. No transfer issued on a transfer. If the passenger must, it conductor demands it, pay fare, and present this transfer with application for redress to Superintendent, B. C. ELECTRIC RY. CO. LTD., Victoria, B. C.

JAN. FEB. MAR. APR. MAY JUN. JUL. AUG. DEC.   **17**   SEP. OCT. NOV.

PERMEATING B.C. ELECTRIC'S CONCERNS IN THE VICTORIA area during 1937 was the fact that its franchise to provide transportation in the city itself would expire on December 5, 1938. The city council was interested in buses or trolley coaches.

A franchise committee, consisting of members of Victoria's city council, was formed, with alderman Archie Wills as chairman. At a meeting with B.C. Electric president W. G. Murrin and vice-president A. T. Goward, Murrin made it clear that

the company did not intend to continue streetcar operation indefinitely after December 5, 1938, but agreed that streetcar operation might be continued for a short time after that date as a matter of convenience while some other form of transportation was being organized, but under no circumstances would the tracks and rolling stock be rehabilitated.

When asked by the franchise committee if the company would consider operating a bus service in place of the streetcars, Murrin replied that such a proposal would only be considered on the basis of a set fare at the outset, and that at a given time, say two or three years, the revenues of the company should be analyzed and if the earnings were not sufficient to pay a fair return on the investment, say 5 percent, then the question of fares should be reviewed. Murrin estimated it would cost in the neighbourhood of $750,000 to put in an adequate bus service in Victoria. He also pointed out that street car operation in Victoria had been unprofitable during the past several years.

In newspaper advertisements, the Street Railwaymen's Union clarified its own position: streetcars would better be able to provide continuing service, should a deteriorating European situation precipitate gas rationing or a rubber shortage.

The buses of Royal Blue Line and Vancouver Island Coach Lines together ran a total bus mileage of 677,500 in 1937, competition indeed for B.C. Electric's Victoria system with its annual streetcar and bus mileage of 1,750,000, despite the restrictions placed upon bus companies. On the Haultain route, Royal Blue Line competed directly with the B.C. Electric, the latter garnering fifty-seven per cent of the riders.

The company's four Haultain bus operators worked weekday shifts of eight hours and forty minutes – seven hours, ten minutes on Sunday – including "dead time" (the time to and from the car barn). The operators had every alternate Sunday off, as well as two week days per month, giving them four days off per month. Their conditions included one week's annual holiday with pay, no pay for sickness, no overtime allowed for Sundays, statutory holidays, or extra trips, and a rate of pay of twenty-five dollars per week. (The seventy-three streetcar operators made 69 cents an hour.)

Thirty-nine streetcars were in operation, a particularly convenient number, since forty could be stored under cover at Pembroke and Cloverdale; room for twelve additional cars in open-air storage was available. The barn at Cloverdale, situated as it was at one of the system's extremities, was now mostly used as dead storage and for the less frequently seen pieces of work equipment.

The Victoria streetcar system consisted of 40.548 miles of single track, 23.408 miles in paved streets, 15.235 in unpaved streets, and 1.905 on private right of way, in car barns, and in yards. Considered by city and municipality, 30.084 miles were in Victoria, 4.152 in

Esquimalt, 3.843 in Oak Bay, and 2.469 in Saanich. More than twelve miles of both 56- and 70-pound rail formed the bulk of the trackage, interlaced, particularly at heavily-travelled intersections, with 60- and 87-pound rail. The total cost of maintaining this system during a recent year had been $37,178.92.

Victoria electors, in their December 1938 civic elections, voted in favour of extending the B.C. Electric franchise.

In an inventory of property taken by the company in 1939, the value of each of the thirty-nine streetcars was carefully noted, as follows:

22, 23	$ 8,837	each
188, 189	9,080	
231 - 240	10,035	
250, 252 - 259	7,922	
381, 383, 387 - 390	8,873	
400 - 409	9,222	

The total value of the streetcars was $357,331, all of them double-enders except the 250s.

Victoria's most magnificent royal celebration commenced as the Canadian Pacific's *Princess Marguerite*, from Vancouver, sailed into Victoria harbour on the evening of Tuesday, May 29, 1939, with its royal passengers, King George VI and Queen Elizabeth. Though rain accompanied their arrival, what everyone would always remember would be the tolling of church bells and the whistles, sirens, bagpipes, and wild cheering that stirred the mind and soul in this, the final moving manifestation of empire.

On Wednesday, a brilliantly sunny day, the royal party visited Victoria's city hall and Oak Bay; in the afternoon, twenty thousand people gathered at Beacon Hill Park to view the presentation of the royal colours to the Royal Canadian Navy Western Command, after which the Navy moved off with its new colours for the four-mile march back to Esquimalt. The royal couple then journeyed west to Hatley Park (Royal Roads) for a late afternoon picnic lunch.

Although streetcar services had been shut down in the morning after 8 a.m. to accommodate the royal visitors, when service resumed, the streetcars flaunted their decorations, bunting and flags, none looking finer in their dress than the neat, trim Birneys.

Thirteen thousand onlookers ringed the harbour on the following morning as the king and queen boarded Canadian National's beautiful *Prince Robert* for the journey to Vancouver, and as it steamed slowly past Ogden Point, five thousand children on the dock sang "Will Ye No' Come Back Again."[44]

On September 10, Canada, at Britain's side again, declared war on Germany. This declaration was all that saved the streetcars for nine more years of service, a brief era that would bring riders to the streetcars in numbers beyond belief; B.C. Electric's Victoria system would be taxed to its limit. The company immediately geared up the Pembroke barn and shop staff for a painting and renovation programme for its streetcars.

On February 14, 1940, necessity dictated the inauguration of a B.C. Electric bus service, a feeder to Esquimalt's naval barracks. A significant element of Victoria's city council still had thoughts of buses, but in June, Esquimalt and Oak Bay municipal councils agreed to keep the streetcars for the time being, Victoria's council unanimously acquiescing.

In June as well, B.C. Electric created a force, working closely with city and provincial police, as well as the Royal Canadian Mounted Police, to guard substations, transmission lines, power plants, and dams, and to monitor gates and entrances on a twenty-

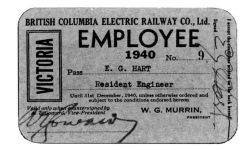

2½M-6-44

BRITISH COLUMBIA ELECTRIC RAILWAY COMPANY, LTD.
VICTORIA, B.C.

STREET RAILWAY
SCHEDULES

WEEKDAY SCHEDULES

OAK BAY, No. 1
FIRST CAR FROM CITY	6.06 a.m.
12-minute service until	11.50 a.m.
10 " " "	7.54 p.m.
12 " " "	11.42 p.m.
LAST CAR FROM CITY	11.42 p.m.
FIRST CAR FROM OAK BAY	6.24 a.m.
12-minute service until	11.50 a.m.
10 " " "	7.48 p.m.
12 " " "	12.00 m.n.
LAST CAR FROM OAK BAY	12.00 m.n.

OUTER WHARF, No. 2
FIRST CAR FROM CITY	6.15 a.m.
20-minute service until	7.52 p.m.
12 " " "	7.55 p.m.
20 " " "	11.55 p.m.
LAST CAR FROM CITY	11.55 p.m.
FIRST CAR FROM OUTER WHARF	6.25 a.m.
20-minute service until	8.07 a.m.
12 " " "	8.05 p.m.
20 " " "	12.05 m.n.
LAST CAR FROM OUTER WHARF	12.05 m.n.

CLOVERDALE, No. 2
FIRST CAR FROM CITY	6.15 a.m.
20-minute service until	7.52 p.m.
12 " " "	7.55 p.m.
20 " " "	11.55 p.m.
LAST CAR FROM CITY	11.55 p.m.
FIRST CAR FROM CLOVERDALE	6.25 a.m.
20-minute service until	8.01 a.m.
12 " " "	8.05 p.m.
20 " " "	12.05 m.n.
LAST CAR FROM CLOVERDALE	12.05 m.n.

BEACON HILL, No. 3
FIRST CAR FROM CITY	6.05 a.m.
20-minute service until	8.04 p.m.
12 " " "	12.05 p.m.
10 " " "	8.05 p.m.
20 " " "	11.45 p.m.
LAST CAR FROM CITY	11.45 p.m.
FIRST CAR FROM BEACON HILL	6.15 a.m.
20-minute service until	8.04 a.m.
12 " " "	12.05 noon
10 " " "	8.05 p.m.
20 " " "	11.55 p.m.
LAST CAR FROM BEACON HILL	11.55 p.m.

FERNWOOD, No. 3
FIRST CAR FROM CITY	6.05 a.m.
20-minute service until	8.10 a.m.
12 " " "	12.05 p.m.
10 " " "	8.05 p.m.
20 " " "	11.45 p.m.
LAST CAR FROM CITY	11.45 p.m.

four-hour basis. This well-trained force would be built up almost entirely of ex-servicemen of every rank.

The upturn in ridership had already taken hold in 1940, as the system-wide figure of 76,411,790 showed: Victoria's streetcar lines had transported 6,830,146, its two bus lines, 568,431, and together they showed the last yearly net loss the system would sustain to the end of streetcar service.

With Canada's west coast sensing its vulnerability, May 22, 1941 was selected, both in Victoria and on the lower mainland, as the date for a first blackout attempt, from 10 p.m. for fifteen minutes. All lights went out all across the region, all streetcars and interurban coaches stood in their tracks, darkened; the successful experiment, repeated, would become more comfortable to everyone.

With the December 7 attack on Pearl Harbor, British Columbians feared that war had arrived on their own shores, and a stringent three-night blackout went into effect the following day. Streetcar and bus service was maintained on a curtailed schedule, with greatly reduced lighting and company personnel at the various route terminals to space the transit vehicles equitably. Automobile lights were painted black.

In 1941 ridership on Victoria's streetcars had increased by more than a million to 7,880,806, while its B.C. Electric buses had carried 797,533. The Victoria system, after years of losses, showed a net profit of $17,254.

As the streetcars were being fitted with metal blackout covers for their headlights, gas rationing went into effect on April 1, 1942, all across Canada. With masses of riders now thronging the streetcars and buses, an unprecedented game plan was in order. To orchestrate B.C. Electric's new transit era, S. Sigmundson, of Winnipeg Electric, was appointed by George S. Gray, Canada's federal transit controller, to the position, newly-minted, of British Columbia's transit controller.

By the end of August, a skip-stop system was in effect, dictated by Sigmundson to speed up traffic. Fully one third of the Victoria area's current streetcar stops were therewith discontinued, but there were signs aplenty to orient riders to their nearest stop.

Not surprisingly, in view of gas and rubber shortages, the Haultain bus line had been discontinued in June although the more strategically-vital Esquimalt feeder bus was retained. Ridership during 1942 was up almost twenty-eight per cent across the system to 107,052,564; in Victoria, 10,251,809 had ridden the streetcars, 873,986, the buses.

Few could have imagined that 1943 would be the last complete year in which Victoria's entire complement of streetcar lines would function. The roller signs on each car, so familiar, listed the system's route designation in the following order:

> Oak Bay
> Outer Wharf
> Cloverdale
> Beacon Hill
> Fernwood
> Esquimalt
> Gorge
> Gonzales
> Hillside
> Uplands
> Burnside
> Mt. Tolmie
> Willows
> Joseph St.
> Special

With electric switch mechanisms removed at three locations, Douglas Street at Burnside Road, Douglas Street at Government

FERNWOOD, No. 3—(Continued)	
FIRST CAR FROM FERNWOOD	6.15 a.m.
20-minute service until	8.10 a.m.
12 " " "	12.05 noon
10 " " "	8.05 p.m.
20 " " "	11.55 p.m.
LAST CAR FROM FERNWOOD	11.55 p.m.

ESQUIMALT, No. 4	
FIRST CAR FROM CITY	6.00 a.m.
15-minute service until	12.00 noon
12 " " "	5.00 p.m.
10 " " "	11.50 p.m.
20 " " "	12.30 m.n.
45 " " "	2.00 a.m.
LAST CAR FROM CITY	2.00 a.m.
FIRST CAR FROM ESQUIMALT	6.22 a.m.
15-minute service until	12.12 noon
12 " " "	5.00 p.m.
10 " " "	12.15 m.n.
20 " " "	12.52 m.n.
45 " " "	2.22 a.m.
LAST CAR FROM ESQUIMALT	2.22 a.m.

GORGE, No. 5	
FIRST CAR FROM CITY	6.05 a.m.
20-minute service until	7.45 a.m.
12 " " "	10.05 a.m.
20 " " "	12.05 noon
12 " " "	8.06 p.m.
20 " " "	11.45 p.m.
LAST CAR FROM CITY	11.45 p.m.
FIRST CAR FROM GORGE	6.25 a.m.
20-minute service until	8.00 a.m.
12 " " "	10.05 a.m.
20 " " "	12.05 noon
12 " " "	8.05 p.m.
20 " " "	12.05 m.n.
LAST CAR FROM GORGE	12.05 m.n.

GONZALES, No. 6	
FIRST CAR FROM CITY	6.00 a.m.
15-minute service until	7.45 a.m.
12 " " "	12.05 noon
10 " " "	7.45 p.m.
15 " " "	11.45 p.m.
LAST CAR FROM CITY	11.45 p.m.
FIRST CAR FROM GONZALES	6.17 a.m.
15-minute service until	7.58 a.m.
12 " " "	12.12 noon
10 " " "	8.02 p.m.
15 " " "	12.02 m.n.
LAST CAR FROM GONZALES	12.02 m.n.

HILLSIDE, No. 6	
FIRST CAR FROM CITY	6.05 a.m.
15-minute service until	8.04 a.m.
12 " " "	12.00 noon
10 " " "	8.05 p.m.
15 " " "	11.50 p.m.
LAST CAR FROM CITY	11.50 p.m.
FIRST CAR FROM HILLSIDE	6.17 a.m.
15-minute service until	8.16 a.m.
12 " " "	12.02 noon
10 " " "	8.02 p.m.
15 " " "	12.02 m.n.
LAST CAR FROM HILLSIDE	12.02 m.n.

UPLANDS, No. 9	
FIRST CAR FROM CITY (to Willows only)	5.56 a.m.
FIRST CAR FROM CITY TO UPLANDS	6.11 a.m.
15-minute service from 6.11 a.m. to 11.41 p.m.	
LAST CAR FROM CITY	11.41 p.m.
FIRST CAR FROM WILLOWS ONLY	6.11 a.m.
FIRST CAR FROM UPLANDS	6.33 a.m.
15-minute service from 6.33 a.m. to 12.03 m.n.	
LAST CAR FROM UPLANDS	12.03 m.n.

Street (Market Street), and Esquimalt Road at Russell Street, Sigmundson's special transportation committee took the first step in creating a smoother flow of streetcar traffic. Reinstalled at Government and Bay streets, Government and Yates streets, and Douglas and Yates streets, a new traffic pattern came into effect in February. Burnside and Gorge streetcars now came from the north into downtown on Government Street, rather than Douglas Street, leaving Douglas Street, inbound, to Esquimalt and Fernwood streetcars.[45] The service improvement was immediately noticeable.

During the month of April, the siding at Dewdney Avenue on the Uplands line, unused since mid-1941, was finally removed, useful salvage for use elsewhere in the system. In the same month, "late cars" began operating on the Gorge, Gonzales, Hillside, Oak Bay, Outer Wharf, and Uplands lines, broadening the territory of "late cars" instituted on January 30 on the Esquimalt route. The Esquimalt cars departed the corner of Douglas and Yates streets at 12:30 a.m., 1:15 a.m., and 2 a.m.

Since Canada's Department of National Defence needed more room on its almost peninsula-like setting, in July B.C. Electric lost, amicably, the last 750 feet of track at its Esquimalt terminus, as well as the streetcar operators' toilet. (Operators were delighted to be allowed, in return, to use the Navy's guard house facility.) Actually, the final two hundred feet of track, with its wye, had been last used on the final day of two-man cars, April 15, 1922. In addition, D.N.D. contributed $900 to the construction of a new loop, thoroughly graded and ballasted, and fitted out with a platform. The war effort indeed!

Since Canada's Selective Service Board had ruled that women could perform as conductors, and only men over forty-five as motormen, the path was open for the company in July to hire women as uniformed "Guides," absolutely essential now in their major role of selling tickets and dispensing information before riders boarded the streetcars. (In Vancouver, eleven women would be hired within the next few months as "conductorettes.")

No one doubted that B.C. Electric had carried as many as 131,619,270 passengers during 1943, and Victoria's streetcars, 13,026,857, their peak performance; the company's nine buses, of which five were in execrable condition, had carried 843,002. The Victoria system showed a net profit of $154,183 for 1943! During the year, the company, under Murrin's direction, had created "The Committee on Post-War Construction," a group charged with planning for transit modernization and conversion to buses.

B.C. Electric's streetcar modernization programme, begun in 1937, began to affect Victorians in May, not only because they had temporarily lost cars 188, 259, 381, 383, 387 and 389, barged across to Vancouver to the rebuilding site, the company's Kitsilano shops, but also because recently rebuilt Vancouver streetcars, 200 and 201, had been sent to Victoria in a sort of exchange. The "new" thirty-three-year-old cars belied their age in every way, quite astonishing Victoria's riders, especially with their rear door's treadle exit. Besides the glistening red and cream paint job, Victorians may have noticed smooth metal flashing over the front and rear bumpers and a modern headlight, but it was the interior that held the revelations: leather-covered, foam-rubber seats, rather than wooden-slat seats; a linoleum floor with non-skid, metal scuff plates rather than wooden-slat flooring; green paint from window sashes to the floor, with natural oak above, rather than dark walnut throughout; a white ceiling; tubular steel stanchions and hand rails, rather than leather straps; a system of heaters; a new buzzer system; and new lighting.

Each of the six cars returned in its modernized form, cars 188 and 259 with their deck roofs levelled to a smoother arch, both having been rebuilt as single-enders. And 200 and 201 stayed, to finish their service in Victoria, two of the more than 150 streetcars extensively rebuilt by the company between 1937 and 1946. (Cars 259 and 389 were back in July, 387 in August, 381 in September, 383 in October, and 188 in November.)

It was on the first day of June 1944 that the dismantling of the streetcar system began, when buses, rather than streetcars, appeared on the Mt. Tolmie line.[46] The line least patronized, without even a passing siding on its twenty-four-block passage of Richmond Avenue, succumbed mainly because its streetcars were needed on the other routes, and because of the dubious condition of its track. The joy-riding experience of careening down the long hill on a city-bound streetcar was in the past, though the track would lie teasingly in its place for some time yet. The dispossessed Burnside line, lightly travelled, carried on, looping in downtown via Government, Yates, and Douglas streets.

Of the terminal-end waiting structures built by the company before World War I, only the one at Gorge Park remained after October, those at the ends of the Esquimalt, Gonzales, Mt. Tolmie, Oak Bay, and Willows lines having been demolished during the month. (Except for the park-keeper's home, all the original Gorge Park buildings had also been levelled by the company.) Though the waiting rooms were hardly needed, what with the frequent war-time headways, they were in need of better maintenance than they had recently received.

B.C. Electric's operators, motormen, conductors, shopmen, and trackmen – except for the personnel of the Chilliwack and Lulu Island lines with their different unions – went on strike on January 9,

1945, not so much against B.C. Electric as the Canadian government which had removed an increase granted in September. Though the strike was termed illegal by the government, a settlement, not particularly satisfactory to the employees, was reached, and streetcars rolled again on the nineteenth.

New buses having arrived, the company on April 10 initiated two new bus services, fanning out from their starting point on Esquimalt Road at Head Street. Six days later B.C.'s regional transit controller, S. Sigmundson, was appointed B.C. Electric's transportation assistant.

A Canada-wide holiday on May 8 celebrated the end of the war in Europe on the previous day. Well timed, the post-war "Report on Transit Operations in Greater Victoria," prepared by H. R. "Roly" Halls, B.C. Electric's transportation assistant in Victoria, was ready on May 22.

Current streetcar service was detailed in the following way:

	Miles of Route	Maximum Number of Regular Cars	Headway (in minutes)
Oak Bay	3.21	4	10 - 12
Cloverdale–Outer Wharf	3.08	3	12 - 20
Beacon Hill–Fernwood	2.84	4	10 - 12 - 20
Esquimalt	3.99	5	10 - 12 - 15
Gorge	3.13	3	12 - 20
Gonzales–Hillside	4.76	6	10 - 12 - 15
Uplands	4.14	3	15
Burnside	1.89	1	20
Total	27.04	29	

Particularly revealing were the figures regarding the quantity of travel on each of the system's eleven individual routes. (The one-time Willows run had been a part of the longer Uplands run, and the loop at the Willows was now used only on special occasions.)

B.C. Electric Railway Co. Ltd.

4775

UPLANDS

		A M P M		HOUR		
		1		15	30	45
		2		15	30	45
		3		15	30	45
		4		15	30	45
		5		15	30	45
		6		15	30	45
		7		15	30	45
		8		15	30	45
		9		15	30	45
		10		15	30	45
		11		15	30	45
		12		15	30	45

JAN. FEB. MAR. APR. MAY JUN. JUL. AUG. DEC. — **9** — SEP. OCT. NOV.

	Trips Per Week	Passengers Per Week
Esquimalt	96	5,647
Gonzales	91	5,136
Oak Bay	96	4,500
Beacon Hill	81	3,311
Hillside	91	2,799
Outer Wharf	76	2,758
Fernwood	81	2,603
Uplands	72	2,516
Gorge	69	2,352
Cloverdale	66	1,501
Burnside	50	861

Passenger business on the Gorge line was still sparse, much as it had been at the line's inception, though boosted by the receipts on one trip in the evening when the Gorge beer parlour closed.

Vigorously competing with B.C. Electric, and holding their own, were the same two bus companies, Blue Line Transit, with eleven buses and three lines, and Vancouver Island Coach Lines, in the greater Victoria area competitively using fourteen buses over four lines. Although they could not pick up or discharge passengers within Victoria's city limits (except at their central terminus, of course), they could, and did, parallel the streetcar lines and served riders in Equimalt, Oak Bay, and Saanich. Extraordinarily, one seven-passenger jitney was still in daily service between downtown and the corner of Quadra Street and Tolmie Avenue. B.C. Electric was operating thirteen buses, numbered V-6 to V-18.

Following are H. R. Halls' conclusions to his detailed report.

Therefore, it is obvious that if the Company is to provide Greater Victoria with an efficient transportation system which will operate at a profit, the street cars will have to be abandoned in favour of a more popular type of vehicle, competing lines will have to be absorbed and the company's modernized system extended into the areas now served by its competitors. Further, if the new system is to attract and retain riders who will otherwise be lost to the automobile, every effort must be made to match the private vehicle in speed, comfort, convenience, and economy, which objectives can best be obtained in Victoria by use of rubber tired vehicles, such as the trolley bus and gasoline motor coach.

Generally, routes operating into the older and more stable residential areas, requiring estimated base headways of fifteen minutes or less, have been recommended for conversion to trolley bus operation, while gasoline buses have been suggested for use on routes requiring less frequent service or routes operating into new and growing districts.

With the rebuilding of car 238 at Vancouver's Kitsilano shop during the year, Victoria's streetcar roster was now in its final configuration: 22, 23, 188, 189, 200, 201, 231 - 240, 250, 252 - 259, 381, 383, 387 - 390 and 400 - 409, twelve cars single-enders. Auxiliary car S.61 and locomotive 906, sometimes used as a tower car, were out of service, stored at Cloverdale barn; with little physical growth of the streetcar system after World War I, the barn on Pembroke Street had been an obvious choice as central barn, the one at Cloverdale being used as a storage shed and yard, mostly for moribund equipment and obsolete single-truck streetcars.

Cash fare was still six cents or six tickets for 35 cents, including transfer in both cases; school tickets sold at ten for 25 cents, and weekly passes were available for one dollar. The above cash fares, tickets, and transfers were also accepted by Blue Line's Haultain, Oak Bay–Uplands, and Shoal Bay bus lines.

According to Halls' report, the streetcar system's trackage statistics were as follows:

miles of main track, single	8.115
miles of main track, *double*	15.217
miles of siding and passing tracks	.175
miles of yard and car-house tracks	.894
miles of track owned	39.618
within Victoria city limits	30.032
outside city limits	9.586
number of sidings and passing track	2
actual route miles of track	23.332

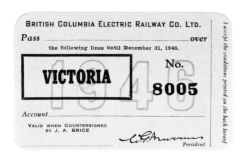

With the end of the war in the Pacific on August 15 it would soon be time for B.C. Electric to begin its post-war transportation renewal programme. (Although it had come into full operation in the fall of 1944, the new steam-turbo unit at Brentwood would have been a greater help if it had been ready sooner.)

It seemed improbable that Victoria could have a transportation system without A. T. Goward, now seventy-three years of age. But he was retiring, to be succeeded as vice-president of B.C. Electric operations by W. C. Mainwaring, with the company since 1932.

Goward, born in Tenby, South Wales, had come to Victoria as a teenager, to be hired by the National Electric Tramway, first for work in the steam plant and then as a streetcar conductor. In 1891, he became a member of the Tramway Company's office staff, and when B.C. Electric took over, manager, and ultimately vice-president. Death would overtake him on June 12, 1946.

In October, one of Seattle's trolley coaches was brought to Victoria to give free rides for a number of days over a route which had been selected to meet a variety of traffic conditions, on Douglas Street north to Queens Avenue, east to Quadra Street, south to Pandora Avenue, and back to Douglas Street. The erection of overhead trolley fixtures and attachments to existing poles had been necessary.

Though hundreds of people rode the trolley coach for a week in November and expressed enthusiasm for its qualities, the greater Victoria area would never have trolley coaches, and for a very simple reason. When the time came to lay out new routes to replace the existing transportation system, the city and municipalities would want too many routes, and certainly not feeders. Trolley coach lines were too expensive to lay out in great profusion; if many lines were desired, they would have to be bus operated, and so they would be.

The main car barn, on Pembroke Street;
Birney 404 strives for the light,
while the sign to the left enjoins operators to
"Drive Slowly When Entering Barn."
AUTHOR'S COLLECTION

The interior of the Pembroke barn,
with only car 384 in evidence.
WALLACE YOUNG PHOTO

The Cloverdale car barn,
with locomotive 906
huddled at the far end.
WALLACE YOUNG PHOTO

Birney 407 in 1934 at
the Outer Wharf terminus
(R. P. Rithet's warehouses
form the background),
poised for the run to Douglas Street
and Cloverdale Avenue.
TED CLARK PHOTO

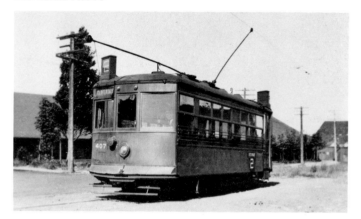

One of the 380-series streetcars
in trouble on Richmond Avenue,
just below the Mt. Tolmie terminus,
in 1929 as the result of a
Halloween prank.
H. R. HALLS PHOTO

The first B.C. Electric bus
on the Victoria system,
servicing its first bus line,
Haultain.
VICTORIA CITY ARCHIVES

Car 23 poses at Mayfair Drive, the terminus of the Mt. Tolmie run, before its return to downtown and the journey out on the Saanich line's Burnside Road.
BOB WEBSTER PHOTO

Car 238 at Kitsilano shop in Vancouver prior to rebuilding in 1945.   TED CLARK PHOTO

Car 238 at Kitsilano shop, shorn of its deck roof, and completely rebuilt, immediately before its return to Victoria. In B.C. Electric's Vancouver system, the cream-painted triangles on either side of the headlight denoted a one-man, front-entrance streetcar.
TED CLARK PHOTO

Douglas Street, north from Yates Street, in the early 1940s.   WALLACE YOUNG PHOTO

Willows car 236 on Fair Street,
running its terminal loop, in September 1946.
W. C. WHITTAKER PHOTO

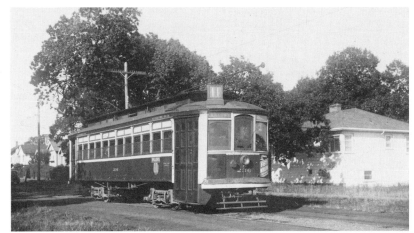

Four months before the demise of Victoria's
streetcars, 387 and 235, running a new lash-up,
"No. 2–Oak Bay–Outer Wharf," meet on Oak Bay
Avenue between Wilmot Place and Hampshire Road.
Car 235 is heading east to Oak Bay.   PABC

New buses for Victoria in 1947.   H. R. HALLS PHOTO

The interior of car 235.
LAWTON GOWEY PHOTO

The interior of car 232.
LAWTON GOWEY PHOTO

The interior of car 238.
LAWTON GOWEY PHOTO

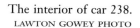

The interior of car 390.
LAWTON GOWEY PHOTO

The interior of car 200
after the end of streetcar service.
LAWTON GOWEY PHOTO

Car 253 on Fort Street,
travelling eastward to the Willows.
STAN F. STYLES PHOTO

Fernwood car 400, travelling east on Yates Street.
Broad Street meets Yates Street in the distance.
TED CLARK PHOTO

Car 403, at the Outer Wharf terminus,
virtually ready to return through downtown
to its Douglas and Cloverdale terminus.
BOB WEBSTER PHOTO

Car 405 on the broad expanse of
the northern reaches of Douglas Street.
BOB WEBSTER PHOTO

Gonzales car 389 on Cook Street,
about to cross Oliphant Avenue.
BOB WEBSTER PHOTO

Gonzales car 381 outbound
on Fort Street, soon to turn southward
on Cook Street.   STAN F. STYLES PHOTO

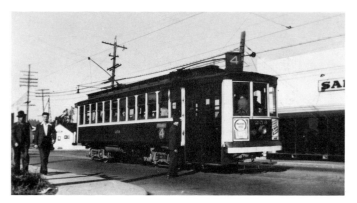

Victoria-bound 258 takes on
a hesitant passenger in front of
the Safeway on Esquimalt Road,
just east of Springfield Street.
TED CLARK PHOTO

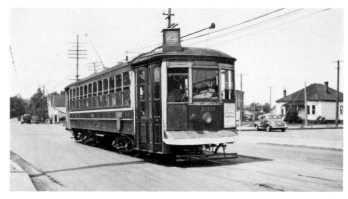

Victoria-bound 390 has just crossed
the E. & N.'s main line,
as has an Esquimalt-bound streetcar,
receding in the distance.   TED CLARK PHOTO

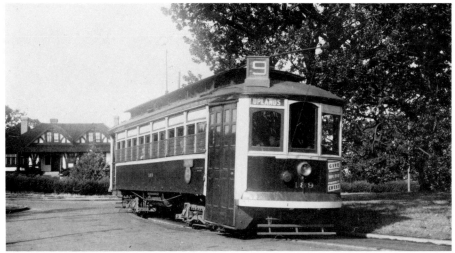

Car 189 circles Midland Circle,
the end of the line for the Uplands run,
in September 1945.
W. C. WHITTAKER PHOTO

Car 406, ready to leave its Cloverdale
terminus, waits on Douglas Street; in the
background, the track turns onto Cloverdale Avenue
for the short distance to the Cloverdale barn.
WALLACE YOUNG PHOTO

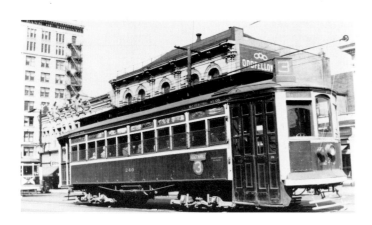

Beacon Hill-bound 240 creates
a powerful impression on
Douglas Street
near Yates Street.
WALLACE YOUNG PHOTO

Burnside car 401 reaches
its terminus on Burnside Road,
former Saanich line territory.
TED CLARK PHOTO

Downtown-bound 387 stops on May Street
at Moss Street on a rare
rainy morning.   VICTORIA CITY ARCHIVES

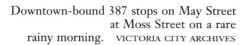

Car 22 crosses Point Ellice Bridge onto Bay Street with "8–Head St." sign, bound for downtown. Canadian National's Victoria yard is visible in the right distance. WALLACE YOUNG PHOTO

Car 383, nearing its Outer Wharf terminus. AUTHOR'S COLLECTION

Heading north on Douglas Street, between Yates and View streets, car 254 shows off its large operator's vestibule, once its roomy, rear "Detroit" platform. FRED HALL PHOTO

Car 255 comes out of its Esquimalt loop for yet another journey through Esquimalt to downtown Victoria.   WALLACE YOUNG PHOTO

Esquimalt car 388 on Douglas Street,
just north of Yates Street.   FRED HALL PHOTO

Although both trolley poles are up,
the nearest will be brought down
in a moment in preparation for
408's return to central Victoria from its
Burnside Road terminus.   TED CLARK PHOTO

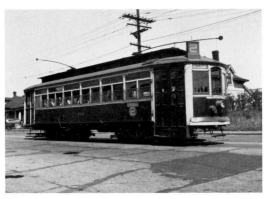

Car 232, developing a sag,
still handsomely represents the
Outer Wharf operation.
TED CLARK PHOTO

Having left Point Ellice Bridge behind, car 239 heads west on Esquimalt Road.
WALLACE YOUNG PHOTO

Car 256 basks in the sun at Gorge Park loop.
WALLACE YOUNG PHOTO

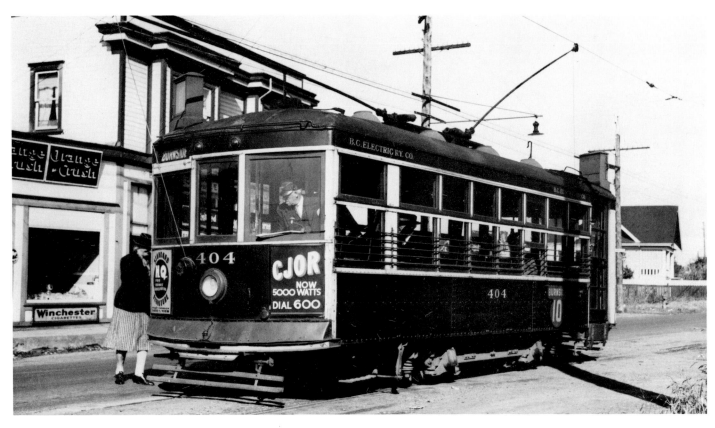

The ten Birneys virtually "owned" the Burnside line during the few post-war years.
W. C. WHITTAKER PHOTO

Esquimalt car 232, eastbound on Esquimalt Road, having just passed Macauley Street.   WALLACE YOUNG PHOTO

Outer Wharf-bound 408 rides along
the causeway in front of the Empress Hotel.
TED CLARK PHOTO

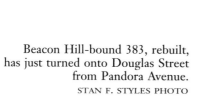

Beacon Hill-bound 383, rebuilt,
has just turned onto Douglas Street
from Pandora Avenue.
STAN F. STYLES PHOTO

Car 389, smartly rebuilt,
swishes the grass of the Uplands line
north of Estevan Avenue.   ERNIE PLANT PHOTO

115

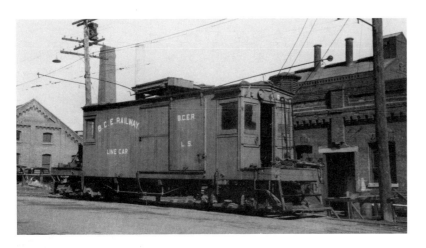

Line car L.5, ready for action,
at Pembroke Street.
WALLACE YOUNG PHOTO

Car 257, looping at the corner
of Windsor Park,
the end of the Oak Bay line.
WALLACE YOUNG PHOTO

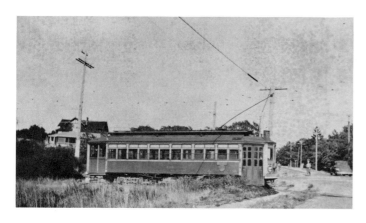

Gonzales car 236 swings onto its loop from Fairfield Road, just short of Foul Bay Road.
PABC

Rebuilt streetcar 201, from Vancouver, nears the end of the Oak Bay line.
W. C. WHITTAKER PHOTO

Cars 200 and 201 arrived, rebuilt, from Vancouver in 1944 and stayed until the end of service. Car 200, on Cadboro Bay Road, works the Uplands line in this photo. Notice the Willows horse racing advertisement.
BOB WEBSTER PHOTO

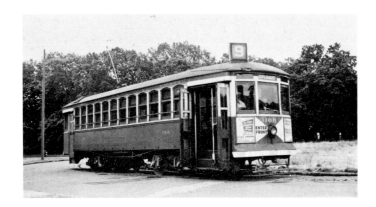

Rebuilt 188 rounds Midland Circle,
the Uplands line's extremity,
for its return to city centre.
Perhaps the photographer will board first.
WALLACE YOUNG PHOTO

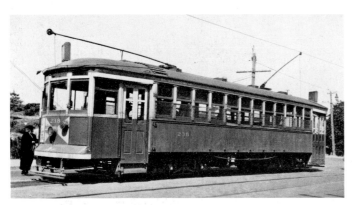

Rebuilt 238 presents a completely different picture
from that of its former classmates, 231-237,
239 and 240, even to having
been lengthened three feet.
WALLACE YOUNG PHOTO

Rebuilt car 387, eastbound
on Superior Street behind the
parliament building, very near the end
of streetcar operations.   WALLACE YOUNG PHOTO

Car 239, on Niagara Street, approaches its
Beacon Hill terminus.   TED CLARK PHOTO

The very last streetcar, 383,
with all guests on board at
Niagara Street at Douglas Street,
prepares to depart for
its farewell run to Pembroke Street
barn. Behind the B.C. Electric's
senior operator, Walter Peddle, is
H. R. "Roly" Halls,
transportation manager, Victoria.
To Peddle's left is E. F. Fox,
B.C. Electric's assistant
public relations director.
Smiling through the window is
Ralph Mathews, executive assistant to
W. C. Mainwaring,
company vice-president,
Victoria.   H. R. HALLS PHOTO

Operator Walter Peddle brings his special car past the Empress Hotel on July 5, 1948, the last day of streetcars.   PABC

The extraordinary decor of 383 for its last trip.   WALLACE YOUNG PHOTO

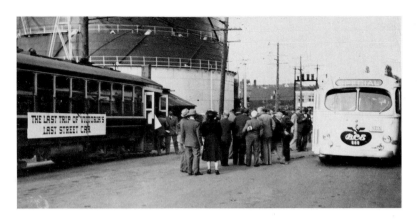

Car 383's arrival at
Pembroke Street barn.
H. R. HALLS PHOTO

The former route of the Gonzales
streetcars is badly askew.   PABC

The report
of the last streetcar operation.
B.C. HYDRO PHOTO

Form T. 1629	**B.C.E.R. Co. Ltd. CAR REPORT CARD**						
Date July-2-48			Barn			Car No. 383	
TIME ON	TIME OFF	LINE	RUN	MILEAGE or HOURS	CONDITION OF CAR	Time Trouble Developed	SIGNATURE OF MOTORMAN & CONDUCTOR
23'07	24'12	O.W	1		O.K.		
					The Final run 7.PM. July 5/48		

A.M. PUT CAR ON No. _____ TRACK   **P.M.** PUT CAR ON No. _____ TRACK

Defects in car equipment must be recorded on card by Motorman. Conductor will also sign card under Motorman's signature. If no defects found mark card O.K. Every car leaving barn must carry a clear card. Card must not be removed by anyone exept person authorized by Mechanical Supt. USE 24 HOUR TIME.

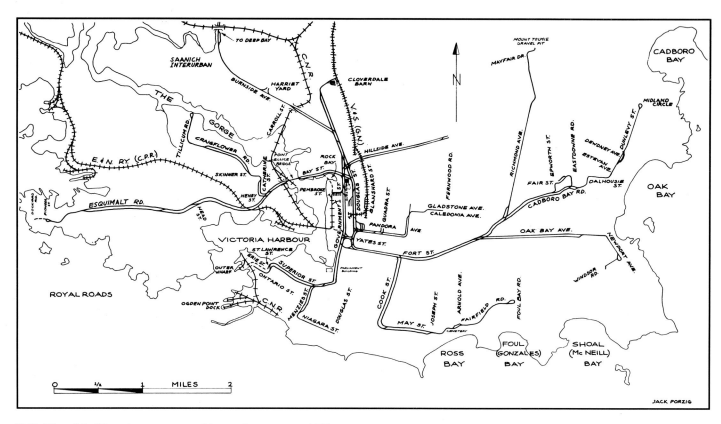

B.C. Electric's Victoria streetcar and interurban system, 1923.

PROPOSED TROLLEY COACH ROUTES

1. Esquimalt - Fernwood
From the Naval Yard gate, via Esquimalt Road, Bay Street, Government Street, Yates Street, Quadra Street, Pembroke Street, Fernwood Road, Haultain Street, looping via Foul Bay Road, Forrester Street and Richmond Road.

2. Gonzales - Hillside.
From a loop of Central Avenue, Hampshire Road and Beaver Street via Victoria Avenue, Beach Drive, Fairfield Road, Cook Street, Fort Street, Douglas Street, Hillside Avenue and Richmond Avenue to a circular loop at Richmond and Cedar Hill Cross Road.

3. Oak Bay - Down Town
From a counter-clockwise loop via Pandora Avenue, Government Street, Fort Street, Douglas Street, via Pandora Avenue, Oak Bay Avenue, Hampshire Road, Central Avenue, Newport Avenue, Oak Bay Avenue, and return.

4. Mount View - Oak Bay
From a counter-clockwise loop via Glanford and Agnes Streets, via Carey Road, Douglas Street, Pandora Avenue, Oak Bay Avenue, Newport Avenue, Central Avenue, Hampshire Road, Oak Bay Avenue and return.
Note: It is probable that the Mt. View half of this line will be a gas bus operation, at least initially.

5. Willows
From a downtown loop of Douglas Street, Yates Street and Government Street, via Fort Street, Cadboro Bay Road and Thompson Avenue to a terminus at Musgrave and Estevan Avenue. Returning via Estevan Avenue, Beach Drive, Bowker Avenue, and Cadboro Bay Road.

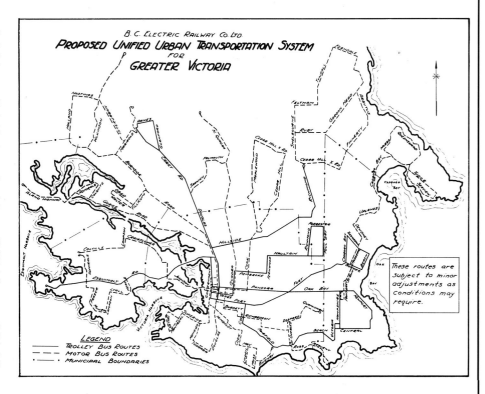

In November, H. R. Halls succeeded A. E. Collis as traffic superintendent, and later transportation manager. Born and educated in Victoria, Halls had been with the company for fifteen years, and had, earlier in the year, written the report on which Victoria's transit system for the second half of the twentieth century would be based.

Although the company had in July wanted to abandon the outer end of the Gonzales line, east from Joseph Street, by running a new bus line into that area, city council had resisted. Thus, when the Fairfield–Gonzales bus line commenced service on November 28, the Gonzales streetcar line also continued to run to its distant, grassy loop at Foul Bay Road.

An oddity of the Gonzales line was its block signal system, with one light at Joseph Street, the end of double track, and the other at the Arnold Avenue siding to the east. When the block signal at Joseph Street displayed red to eastbound streetcars, they waited for the inbound car to arrive at Joseph Street onto the double track. When the Birneys had been introduced on the line as short-run cars to Joseph Street only, the company had introduced the block light system because of the increased movements and the confusion that could be caused as the Birneys came onto single track to reverse to run back into downtown. A further unique feature of the Gonzales operation was the use of metal (rather than wooden) staffs on the Arnold Avenue–Foul Bay Road segment.

The complete Victoria transit system had carried even more passengers in 1945 than in the previous year, 11,955,582 on the streetcars and 1,789,413 on the buses. Yet another ridership record had been set by the total B.C. Electric transportation network, with 144,376,774.

On April 26, 1946, company president William George Murrin retired from his post, to be replaced by Albert Edward "Dal" Grauer, the sixth head of B.C. Electric, and its last, as events of the future would reveal. Three days earlier, company and municipal officials had been driven around the greater Victoria area on a new Canadian Car Brill City-type bus which the company was proposing for its new bus and trolley coach system.

The maximum speed allowable for streetcars was increased by fifty per cent on June 22 to eighteen miles per hour. Further amendments by the provincal government included the following: the number of standees was not to exceed fifty per cent of a street-car's capacity during non-rush hour, streetcars were to reduce speed on downgrades and be kept under instant control, and no un-authorized person would be henceforth tolerated in the motorman's vestibule.

The Esquimalt streetcar line lost its western extension on August 18 with the cutting back to Head Street of the line's regular operation. From this date, the only streetcars operating to the Esquimalt loop were the specials at 7:15 a.m. and 7:30 a.m. from downtown Victoria for dockyard workers, and the one daily return from Esquimalt at 4:30 p.m., 12:30 p.m. on Saturday. In addition, the Head Street cars, which would display that destination's sign below the motorman's window, were through-routed with the Burnside line, via Douglas, Yates, and Government streets; No. 4 existed no longer, while No. 8 was plucked out of the past as the number for the Head Street run. At the same time, bus service commenced from Broad and Yates streets via Johnson Street Bridge to Esquimalt.

All through the summer, as if in defiance of the inexorable move to buses, the men at Pembroke street barn and shop were especially active, not only whitewashing its ceiling and beams, but also refurbishing and repairing many of the 230- and 250-class streetcars, especially 255, 256 and 258. The Department of Railways' Chief Inspector, Robert E. Swanson, had found only cars 231, 234, 238, 403 and locomotive 905 in good order, and had complained to Deputy Minister J. M. Stewart that "the interior of the city streetcars was found to be in very dirty condition, and I would suggest that steps be taken by the Company to have the floors more thoroughly cleaned and swept out in future as they do not appear to me to be in a fit sanitary condition for the transportation of the general public."[47]

On September 3, B.C. Electric purchased the Victoria (and Nanaimo) interests of Blue Line Transit Company, twenty-nine buses and ninety employees becoming part of the company. Halls stated that "the company would continue using all buses obtained from the Blue Line until they are able to proceed with plans for trolley coaches." (Victoria's city council had on May 14 rejected Blue Line's proposal to operate the transit system in Victoria. On July 15, Vancouver's city council had rejected Blue Line's bid for a transport licence there!)

Alderman H. M. Diggon, chairman of the Greater Victoria Transportation Committee, presented terms of the specifications for the unified transportation system for greater Victoria to city council for final ratification on October 15, before presenting them to the other municipalities. Included in the specifications for the twenty-year franchise were provisions for the discontinuance of the streetcar system within eighteen months and payment of $650,000 by the successful company towards the cost of streetcar track removal. The *Colonist* newspaper's two sub-headlines in regard to the specifications captured the essence of why trolley coaches would

☛ *Read the Facts the*
WHEN YOU VOTE NEXT

✔ LOWEST FARES

A weekly $1.00 pass or four tickets for 25 cents and universal transfers on all lines of Victoria, Esquimalt, Oak Bay and all that portion of Saanich lying roughly within a 3½-mile circle of the City Hall. Children under five years free; other children 8 tickets for 25 cents.

A special fare of three tickets for 25 cents covering Ten Mile Point, a portion of Gordon Head and the Burnside-Wilkinson Road area, with transfers good anywhere in the system.

With the inclusion of the $1.00 pass, this provides a lower fare structure than any other city of comparative size in Canada.

✔ CITY TO SHARE EARNINGS

The companies are to pay to the municipalities three per cent of all the money paid by the public as fares.

Let's Settle this Matter On

never appear: "Provision Made for Trolley Buses" and "Municipalities Will Designate Stops."

When the city and the municipalities called for tenders for a unified system in October, B.C. Electric was, not surprisingly, the only bidder; in Saanich, Vancouver Island Coach Lines bid.

When voters went to the polls – December 12 in Victoria and December 14 in Esquimalt and Oak Bay – to cast their ballots in regard to the bylaw to grant B.C. Electric an inter-municipal transportation franchise, they turned it down; a three-fifths majority was missed by fewer than seven hundred votes. The buses ordered went to North Vancouver.

Late in the year, Birney 402, involved in a collision, had been permanently taken out of service; by early February 1947, three more Birneys were out of service, for sale, stripped of any part the company could use for repairs on the six remaining Birneys.

"The old streetcars are to be removed once and for all," trumpeted the newspaper ads inserted by the Greater Victoria Transportation Committee. Saanich was part of the package this time around and Vancouver Island Coach Lines had partnered itself with B.C. Electric, two steps up in credibility for the public's perception of a unified system. The voters in the city and the three municipalities voted in the affirmative on June 19 for the new twenty-year franchise which was to go into effect on November 1 and give B.C. Electric eighteen months to withdraw streetcar service. The company would pay $250,000 to Victoria, $35,000 to Esquimalt, and $25,000 to Oak Bay to assist with the estimated $600,000 cost of track removal.

The No. 5 Gorge and No. 8 Head Street lines were the first two shut down, offering their last service in the early morning of July 1.[48] In terms of trackage terminated, all streetcar track on Bay Street west from Douglas Street out to Esquimalt and to Gorge Park had been closed down, as had the eastern seven-tenths of a mile of the Uplands line on grassy private right-of-way, north of Estevan Avenue. No more would the operator and his streetcar circle the picturesque loop around Midland Circle, stopping just before regaining the straight track so that the operator could re-line the switch with his switch iron for the return trip. Capital Iron in Victoria would acquire the streetcar system's removed rails, except for those at Midland Circle which merely had their heads sliced off, the rest of the rails and their bases still malingering today under the pavement.

With the Head Street line gone, Burnside was linked with Uplands with a fifteen-minute service, beginning July 1; Uplands cars showed number 9, Burnside, 10. As if it was another era, special cars had run on the afternoon of June 30 to the Willows fairgrounds, actually for the very last time. Within two weeks, the first track removed was that of the Gorge loop, on company property, to make way for the buses. Victoria city council made the decision about the next track to be lifted, 350 feet of double track on the Gorge line's Henry Street; the city saw Henry Street as a test section to ascertain costs of track removal, and work began on October 9.

The longest transportation strike in the history of British Columbia, twenty-nine days, came to an end on November 17 as B.C. Electric's 2,800 members of the Street Railwaymen's Union (A.F.L.) voted 2,169 to 360 to return to work. They had sought an increase of twenty cents an hour, but accepted fifteen cents; their desire for a forty-hour work week had been rejected, leaving them with their previous forty-six.

The company's streetcars and buses were operating again on November 18, and the new franchise, delayed by the strike, would

The Buzzer

Published by the British Columbia Electric Railway Co.

Vol. 31   VICTORIA, MONDAY, APRIL 7, 1947   No. 45

First Hundred Years the Hardest

BIRTHDAYS are associated by the young of our species with parties at which ice cream, cake and subsequent tummy aches are available ad lib, and at which presents of fabulous worth are expected. As time goes on, birthdays lose their glamor, come into effect on December 1. On that day, new buses and new fares would go into effect. The cash fare would be seven cents, or four tickets for twenty-five cents, and a weekly pass would be up to $1.25. Transfers, under the new franchise, would be interchangeable within a three-and-a-half-mile circle between B.C. Electric and Vancouver Island Coach Lines.

The early hours of December 1 saw the last of the streetcars on the Gonzales–Hillside, Estevan–Burnside, and Cloverdale lines.[49] Later that day, only sixteen streetcars were still in service – no Birneys – and on the following three routes: No. 1, Oak Bay; No. 3, Beacon Hill–Fernwood; and Outer Wharf–Willows, a new hook-up, with Outer Wharf cars showing No. 2, Willows cars showing No. 11, and operating via Government, Yates, Douglas, and Fort streets. The Willows designation was thereby reintroduced with the abandonment of the Uplands line between the Willows and Estevan Avenue. All track on Douglas Street north of Pandora Avenue, including Cloverdale barn's, was out of service, and the track on Government Street from Yates Street north to Pembroke Street was utilized only by the streetcars leaving or returning to the car barn. These December 1 abandonments reduced greater Victoria's streetcar track mileage to 18.28, or 10.09 route miles; and so the unified system was in place, with fifty-five buses and streetcars out on the streets during rush hours.

During 1947, Bay Street substation had been modernized and twenty-six new buses had arrived for December 1 service. Passengers carried during the year totalled 16,573,946, including those transported by Blue Line: across B.C. Electric's system a record 156,416,742 riders had been accommodated.

Victoria's final streetcar year got underway ironically with the beginning of track removal on the Esquimalt line from the dockyard end in early January. The diamond crossing with the E. & N. was also removed at this time.

When the Willows streetcar line operated its last complete day on January 31, 1948, car 232 making its final journey, only three lines were left. Beginning on February 1, the Outer Wharf and Oak Bay lines were joined, creating a different No. 2 run; and the No. 3 Beacon Hill–Fernwood was still doing business. The roller-coaster-like track on the causeway in front of the Empress Hotel was still rocking its streetcars, but it had been the Birneys which had bounced best.

Oak Bay car 231 received its own pummelling on March 2 when it collided vehemently on Oak Bay Avenue with a heavy truck that was being towed. There were no serious injuries, and there was no sense in repairing the streetcar.

With the coming of March, track removal became serious, with a California company, Francher & Francher, having been awarded the contract for lifting the rails. Trolley wire had already been in the process of being removed since January. The Esquimalt and Nanaimo Railway had been concerned about the track on Store Street between Chatham and Discovery streets which it shared jointly with B.C. Electric, but it would stay, necessary for the industries it served.

It was in the early Sunday hours of May 16 that the last Fernwood and Oak Bay streetcars rolled into Pembroke barn, their historic routes done forever with streetcars. This penultimate abandonment action left but two lines, including one of the first four of the National Electric Tramway. The Outer Wharf and Beacon Hill lines reinstituted service on Government Street between Yates and Pembroke streets after a five and a half months' hiatus. Their shuttle routes and schedules were simple: five-minute service was provided

This pass went into effect immediately after the end of streetcar operation.

between the northern terminus at Pembroke Street and the junction at Menzies and Superior streets, with ten-minute service from the junction to the two outer termini, as the two streetcar runs went their separate ways. Cars 381, 383 and 387 were most often seen in this final flourish of streetcars.

The last streetcar act concluded just after midnight, early Sunday, July 4, 1948, as fifty-eight years of streetcars in greater Victoria ended with the shutting down of the Beacon Hill and Outer Wharf lines. The Victoria *Times* on Saturday had reminded readers that the Outer Wharf run, along with the Beacon Hill line, provided the last local opportunity residents would have to ride a streetcar. "But there will be many today who view with regret the passing of the old cars. There was a homeliness and familiarity about them that had its own attraction – a dowdy dignity that the streamlined buses cannot match. A certain sadness accompanies their disappearance. Old Victoria has changed a little more."

Festooned with cartoons of weeping streetcars and a large sign on each side reading "The Last Trip of Victoria's Last Street Car," car 383 made one last trip, empty, on Monday, July 5, from Pembroke Street barn to the east end of Niagara Street at Beacon Hill Park, where it picked up almost a hundred last day "mourners" who had been brought to that point by buses and returned them, non-stop, to the Pembroke Street barn. The last day's special guests, including transportation manager H. R. Halls (whose father, S. J. Halls, B.C. Electric's once manager of the light and power department, had been a special guest on the first Saanich line trip), sat and stood amid streamers of black crepe paper and humorous slogans while operator Walter Peddle made the most of one more opportunity with one of the handsome Preston cars. Upon the car's arrival at the barn, mementos were there for the taking, even the

In 1949, B.C. Electric reversed its colour scheme, cream becoming the base colour, and simultaneously introduced its new BCE symbol, above, strikingly red. (Only a few of Vancouver's P.C.C. streetcars acquired the new bus-intended paint job.)

operator's stool ending up in someone's rec room. Less than half a block from where car 3 had clanged rather nervously on a chilly February morning more than fifty-eight years earlier, car 383 came home to close the era of the streetcars in Victoria. Even the day's proposal of preserving car 22 went unnoticed, unremarked.

Tuesday's *Daily Colonist* reported that the memorial "services were held late yesterday afternoon for one of the city's most tireless workers during the past 60 years – Victoria's last streetcar."

On hand for the brief but simple ceremony, held in the Langley Street office of the B.C. Electric Railway Co., were members of the City Council, the mayors and reeves of surrounding municipalities, directors of the Chamber of Commerce, directors of the Victoria and Island Publicity Bureau, representatives of the press, B.C. Electric officials and employees.

The group of "mourners" numbered nearly 100 as W. C. Mainwaring, vice-president of the company, passed among them with expressions of sympathy at the passing of "this monument of public transportation."

Despite the heavy tugs of memory there were no tears shed at the ceremony which lasted nearly an hour. Then the "mourners" were transported by bus to the old Beacon Hill terminus. Standing there at the end of the line was the "last of the Mohicans," somberly decorated for the solemn occasion. With the "mourners" jam-packed aboard, just as crowds of Victoria citizens had been wont to do in the rush hours of an earlier day, the cortege moved through the city to the car barns on Pembroke Street where "interment" followed.

Surviving is a bright and shiny family of motor buses which run over 68 miles of streets in Greater Victoria.

The fairground buildings remaining at Willows exhibition grounds, including the race track, went up in flames during the same year as the streetcars' demise. The land was soon subdivided, and today nothing remains of this former land of excitement and pleasures, so inextricably linked with streetcar days and another world of simpler pursuits.

Art Stott, the long-time editorial writer of the *Victoria Times*, wrote a day after the ceremonial journey of 383:

It ends with a jolt, this last trolley ride. It has the finiteness of the last period at the close of the last sentence in the book. There isn't any more. And the streetcar, having disgorged its final load of privileged passengers from this post-scheduled run, clatters off into limbo. With it goes an era.

The streetcar has been an inanimate thing, often cursed, seldom blessed. But it has been part of the warp and woof of an age, the willing though abused servant of an impatient public, a faithful vehicle despite all the derision that has been heaped upon it.

Now it has ended its life of usefulness. Those who attach to it the events of their days will look henceforth only at its skeleton, the trolley-diner, startling in garish paint and filled with the odors of cooking – a thing immobile. And though its departure may add something to urban tranquility, it leaves its former patrons not without wistfulness for the clanging, banging times in which it ran.

Car 406, "The Jolly Trolley," now gone, but once a powerful attraction for children.
PABC

Epilogue

NOT ONLY AS TROLLEY-DINERS, BUT ALSO AS CHICKEN houses, outhouses, hamburger stands, and even homes, Victoria's streetcars somehow commanded a broader landscape than ever. B.C. Electric had begun advertising their sale as long ago as July 1947 – the Birneys going for $100, the wooden cars for $150 – and by late summer of 1948, they were as far afield as Parksville, with a pair of them together functioning as a home at Luxton, one at Langford as the "Night Owl" diner (complete with "Esquimalt" destination sign), and another in the Fernwood area of Victoria as a greenhouse. Birney 401 gained considerable fame as "The Jolly Trolley" on Tattersall Drive in Saanich as a children's mini-theatre and much-loved play area, part of Mrs. Gertrude McGill's Co-operative Play Group, even to being filmed by Fox, MGM and Paramount.

Others went to Colwood (car 22), Saanichton, Mount Newton Cross Road, Goldstream, Sooke and Lake Cowichan (car 400); car 254 and another performed bunkhouse duty for Summit Lumber Company (between Duncan and Cowichan Lake) and car 256 became the lunchroom for the employees at the brickyard on the site of today's Mayfair Shopping Centre.

Those streetcars unsold by October 8 were towed on that day by an E. & N. 0-6-0 steam locomotive from Pembroke barn south on

Store Street and across Johnson Street Bridge to the E. & N.'s Victoria West yard, where they were incinerated, among them car 383, showing number 4 route sign still with its "Last Street Car" banners. Neither locomotive 905 nor any of the streetcar system's maintenance and work equipment survived the conflagration.

Francher & Francher was back at work in April 1949, beginning the removal of twenty-five miles of track, a task that would be completed by summer, the first anniversary of streetcar-less travel. Eleven transit routes were being serviced by eighty buses: 47 Brills, 16 Macks, 14 Fords, two Ford school buses, and a Mercury school bus.

Pembroke Street barn was now a bus garage, accommodating as well a major repair shop, body and paint shop, unit overhaul centre, stores and offices. The Garbally Road bus garage, completed in November of 1948 at a cost of $300,000, was responsible for servicing, inspections, washing and light repairs.

H. R. Halls was transportation manager, and E. W. Arnott, with more than thirty-eight years of experience in the field of transit, was vice-president in charge of Vancouver Island operations. W. C. Mearns was responsible for the maintenance of the buses, and Guy Barclay was mechanical superintendent.

British Columbia's one non-B.C. Electric streetcar operation, Nelson Street Railway Company, fell to buses almost a year after Victoria's system, on June 20, 1949.

In 1950, B.C. Electric acquired the Saanich bus operations of the Vancouver Island Coach Lines, and the same year, not without reason, carried what still stands as the greatest number of passengers carried by the greater Victoria system in a twelve-month period, 17,535,723.

Seven years later, the first Canadian Car and Foundry and General Motors diesel buses began arriving for B.C. Electric service, thereby signalling a gradual phasing-out of the wave of buses which had arrived to supplant the streetcars.

Eleven years after the demise of the streetcars, C. B. Fisher in the *Daily Colonist* brought the trolley era to life through discussion with some of the men who had kept the streetcars rolling.[50] George Thompson of Beechwood Avenue summed up 41 years of driving and conducting from 1912 to 1953:

I used to get a big kick out of it. I never went out with a chip on my shoulder. Those British sailors at Esquimalt in 1912 were a great bunch of boys. Gave us support when we had trouble with rowdies. Never had much money. We used to get a bottle of beer for five cents from their canteen at the end of the run, plus tobacco duty-free.

I started at 22 cents an hour, 10 hours a day, 365 days a year. There was a very strong seniority in those days.

They had very small cars when I started, with hand brakes. It was different 40 years later. I had a huge crowd on one night, and a couple of fellows tried to guess how many. One counted 134, the other 137!

In the early years we acted as transfers for the merchants. Dixie Ross, the big grocer, would come out with a load of provisions and ask us if we could drop it off at such and such a corner. We got 15 cents and some housewife got her groceries faster. We did the same with meat and liquor.

In the early boom days in Victoria around 1912 a good many of the roads were poorly built and consequently the tracks didn't have the foundation they should've had. This was one reason why the cars used to sway when travelling fast. After the boom, when things grew more stable, the city demanded better roads from its contractors. It was then that Pandora Avenue was laid down, and the rails on that street were to me the best in the city.

Old Jack Dempsey was one of the most respected of conductors. Never raised his voice, even at union meetings. He was always the same, a gentleman. Died at 91 a few years ago.

Charlie Wharton, chief maintenance man for thirty years at the Pembroke Street barn, said that he doubted if there was a better bunch of mechanics anywhere. A few of us had to be able to spot the trouble instantly when a car broke down on the run. We had to decide within a minute or so of diagnosis whether it should go back to the barn or continue on.

We were called out at all hours and weather. I would wake my crew up around midnight and ride the wrecking car out to where one of the trams had jumped the track. We would jack it up, then pull 20 tons over a boiler plate onto the rails.

Every streetcar had a personality. When one broke down on the run I could almost guess the trouble when they told me the number of the car. It was tough going even in the barns. It was mostly overhead work. There were miles of piping on a single car and air valves were the toughest things to fix. We had to work in bitter weather, freezing cold in the open sheds on Pembroke Street.

Cars were brought in for inspection every 1,300 miles. After 200,000 miles a car was completely overhauled. Every bolt was inspected with a hammer. We never took any chances. On the smaller runs, if anything happened within the 1,300 miles it was a black mark for the inspector. Some of the cars ran millions of miles. Old 235 made in New Westminster, ran well over 10,000,000 miles.

A man had to be master of several trades to know a streetcar through and through and be able to fix it. I used to be a fitter in the shipyards. When they closed down after the First Great War I entered the B.C. Electric shops. After a lot of hard work and study I was able to fix anything on a streetcar.

The cars had a good safety record. If the conductor fainted, the circuit would break because the control hand would rise and the emergency brake would go on instantly. The car would stop in a few feet. It was called the dead man's control.

Streetcar operator Charlie Croft remembered that

once when passing Foul Bay Road, a little child ran out from behind a car directly in front of my car. I shut the power off instantly and the brakes slammed on so suddenly I thought we were off the track. The child's life was saved by a couple of feet.

The oldest surviving operator in 1959 was ninety-one-year-old Oliver Snaith, who still played a "mean game of crib" and took "a constitutional every day as far as Beacon Hill" from his home at the Westholme Hotel.

Streetcars were very permanent. You could direct people easily. You knew where they were going. We had our bits of trouble. A good many cars used to cut in front of us. One day in "the Dardanelles" a person tried it and got sandwiched between one of our cars and a telephone post. Lucky he wasn't hurt, but the car was a wreck.

In the early days some of the passengers used to proffer ten-dollar gold pieces and ask for the change. Around 1905 this was like giving a fellow a $100 bill to change. We couldn't make it, and I guess they got a free ride.

When the company sold passes some people would heave them through the window and a wife or friend would board the same car. You couldn't watch everything. A while later the company acknowledged receipt of 50 cents conscience money.

Oak leaves were dangerous, full of slime. Used to skid the cars off the track. Kids were a nuisance, too. Some pretty big kids out of the kid stage used to pull the trolley off the wire.

I started in June of 1897. Before that I drove for Bray's and Victoria Transfer. Went over the Point Ellice Bridge half an hour before that May 24 [*sic*] tragedy when the streetcar fell through.

On British Columbia's mainland, torching streetcars was a regular feature of the company's Kitsilano shop in Vancouver between October 1948 and February 1955. All the Victoria streetcars which finished their careers in Vancouver were scrapped by having their bodies pushed off their trucks and set afire. Indeed, during these six-plus years, 366 streetcars, interurban coaches, and work vehicles were destroyed at Kitsilano in this manner!

Former Victoria sightseeing car 123 operated the special final Vancouver sightseeing trip, for B.C. Electric and civic officials, on September 17, 1950, while former Saanich interurban coach 1242, renumbered to 1316, was the lead coach of a two-car train (with 1304, now in a museum at Glenwood, Oregon) which operated the last run on the Central Park line – once Westminster & Vancouver Tramway – on July 16, 1954. The six Saanich coaches, renumbered, respectively, from 1239 - 1244 to 1313 - 1318, had been part of the fleet of fourteen interurban cars which had provided service on this line to the last day; only one interurban line in Canada and

"Trolley Diner," one use for
a dispossessed streetcar.   BOB WEBSTER PHOTO

The interior of "Trolley Diner,"
greenery and the smell of coffee.   PABC

Two Victoria streetcars huddle closely to form a home.   PABC

Car 233, precariously positioned for domestic use.   PABC

Former Saanich line baggage-express
coach 1706 in 1949 at Chilliwack
on Canada's longest interurban line.
ERNIE PLANT PHOTO

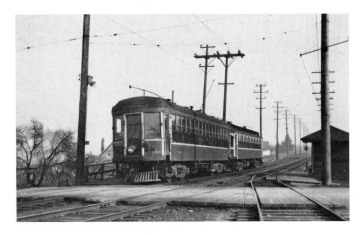

Former Saanich line interurban coach 1244,
renumbered to 1318, but with both
Saanich pilots still intact,
leads 1307 past Lakeview station on the
Central Park line in 1953.   AUTHOR'S COLLECTION

Interurban coach 1315, ex-Saanich line 1241,
on the Central Park line in 1954.
ALLAN PRESCOTT PHOTO

After streetcars, looking north on Douglas Street from Johnson Street.
B.C. Electric's office at the Pandora Avenue corner, behind which
Saanich interurban cars once reposed, is strikingly visible. PABC

the United States would provide more than the sixty-three years of service that the old Tramway route had – Oregon's Portland–Oregon City route.

When the Saanich interurban coaches had been renumbered in 1929 and 1930, the company had installed larger motors, removed the toilet facility from each coach, and replaced the heavy wooden pilots with a lighter type of fender. Nonetheless, coaches 1315 and 1318 betrayed their Saanich-line heritage to the end, 1315 somehow retaining its roof-top toilet ventilator, and 1318 keeping both its majestic, heavy railroad pilots. All six were scrapped at Kitsilano between September 1954 and February 1955.

Baggage express car 1706, so long a fixture on the Chilliwack line, had assisted contractor Hume & Rumble in the removal of trolley wire on that dieselized line, succumbing to the scrapper's torch on January 30, 1952. Car 1707, briefly on the Saanich line, had spent its latter years as a maintenance-of-way car on the Chilliwack line; badly damaged in a collision in March 1956, it was scrapped later in the year. Car 1501, renumbered 1216 – its mail compartment converted to seating space – remained in regular service on the Steveston line until its scrapping in September 1958.

B.C. Electric's last streetcar in regular service was one of its thirty-six streamlined P.C.C.s, numbered 424, on Vancouver's No. 14 – Hastings East run in the morning of April 22, 1955. The company's last regular interurban run occurred in the early morning of February 28, 1958, as car 1225, virtually identical to the Saanich six, made its way out to Steveston from Marpole, and return, about eight miles each way.

The fabulous near-decade, 1905 to 1914, had been brought intensely to mind in 1956 with the death on July 5 of Rochfort

Henry Sperling, B.C. Electric's general manager during those exhilarating years.

Under the terms of the Power Development Act, the B.C. Electric Company Limited was appropriated by the province of British Columbia on August 1, 1961. (The B.C. Electric Railway Company Limited's assets had been acquired by the B.C.E. Co. Ltd. on January 2 in a simple paper transaction.) A. E. "Dal" Grauer, appointed to the new position of chairman of the board on December 29 (H. L. Purdy had become president), died six days before the expropriation.

On March 30, 1962, the former B.C. Electric operations became the B.C. Hydro and Power Authority, with the freight-hauling interurban lines a separate operation, B.C. Hydro Rail (Southern Railway of B.C. today), but still retaining – indeed, to this day – a logo including the identifying tag, "the BCE route".

On April 1, 1979, B.C. Hydro and Power Authority's interurban bus operations became the domain of Pacific Coach Lines, and exactly one year later, B.C. Hydro shucked off its bus and trolley coach operations, in accordance with the provisions of the Urban Transit Authority Act and the Metro Transit Operating Company Act. The new entity was called the Urban Transit Authority and Metro Transit Operating Company, with 662 buses, 311 trolley coaches, and two 400-passenger catamarans crossing on Burrard Inlet between Vancouver and North Vancouver.

The British Columbia Electric Railway Company Limited ended its eighty-six-year life, being dissolved on May 10, 1983, the climax of a process initiated more than twenty-three years earlier.

Amendments to the B.C. Transit Act brought an expanded B.C. Transit into being on June 1, 1985. Metro Transit Operating Company, which had operated transit in greater Victoria and greater Vancouver, was thereby merged into B.C. Transit, which had operated transit in other B.C. areas.

This comprehensive orchestration of B.C.'s transit services served as a prelude to the inauguration of regular service on January 3, 1986 of the 13.2-mile Advanced Light Rapid Transit line (A.L.R.T., dubbed SkyTrain) between Vancouver and New Westminster, most of it constructed high above the old Westminster and Vancouver Tramway right-of-way. After an hiatus of almost twenty-eight years, an interurban railway line was once again moving thousands of riders in British Columbia. Extended farther into New Westminster, SkyTrain on March 19, 1990 commenced full regular service on a further extension across the Fraser River to Surrey.

In greater Victoria, traces of B.C. Electric's streetcar and interurban operations are easy to find. The Saanich line's right-of-way beyond Burnside Road is covered, appropriately, by Interurban Road, and three major tell-tale dips in the roadway indicate the locations of the Saanich line's three trestles: first trestle, at Charlton Road; second trestle, almost immediately north near Alan Road; and third trestle, north of Goward Substation and the Interurban Campus of Camosun College at Viaduct Avenue.

From Goward Road, the line is especially tangible, following the west side of West Saanich Road as a gravel road to Wallace Drive. Wallace Drive is now Saanich line's right-of-way, the power poles still in place along Wallace Drive giving the route a particularly evocative interurban line ambiance. North of Saanichton, the right-of-way becomes Aldous Terrace (on the east side of Sansbury School) and, at Bazan Bay, Mainwaring Road; immediately north of the airport, Wilson Road occupies the right-of-way, and north from Highway 17A, Tatlow Road occupies the Saanich line directly to

Deep Bay, now Deep Cove once again, as it was before the arrival of the Saanich interurban line.

Immediately south of the Deep Cove terminus, The Chalet still looms and lures handsomely, now as one of the finest restaurants on Vancouver Island.

The lengthy gravel pit spur can be easily followed from the southeast corner of Stelly's Secondary School grounds on Wallace Drive, south on the west side of Graham Creek, and the gravel pit itself, south of Keating Cross Road is a powerful central Saanich presence yet. As late as the 1940s, it had still been possible to find some of the station shelters, such as Mallowmot, on site.

In downtown Victoria, B.C. Electric's former head office building still holds down the southwest corner of Fort and Langley streets, but it is the northern end of Store Street which holds the most fascination. The 1892 powerhouse still creates a powerful impression, assisted by the initial eight-track building of the Pembroke Street car barn and two associated buildings on the north side of Pembroke Street. The E. & N. track still comes up Store Street from its route across the Johnson Street Bridge, which itself betrays its pulled-up tracks, filled in with blacktop at the bridge's east end. A mere three blocks north of Pembroke Street at Government and Bay streets, Bay Street substation still broods in art-deco splendour.

On the way to Uplands, a visit to the magnificent home of the streetcar system's progenitor, David W. Higgins, is not to be missed, its destruction happily thwarted by Mr. Carl Rudolph, its purchaser and restorer. In Uplands, at Midland Circle (Midland and Ripon roads) where streetcars once picturesquely looped, track may be found, surreptitiously, by a careful examination of the grassy southern perimeter of the circular roadway.

Of the streetcars only number 400 remains, very much alive on the tourist trolley line in Nelson, inaugurated on July 1, 1992. Until recently, a visit to mainland British Columbia would have revealed Birney 400, painstakingly restored, on display at the B.C. Transportation Museum in Cloverdale, twenty-five miles east of Vancouver. Found in 1970 near Lake Cowichan, it was restored by May 1973 and presented to the B.C. Provincial Museum, which displayed it for a time outside the museum in Victoria. Having undergone further restoration on the mainland to bring its appearance as close as possible to that which it presented to Victorians, car 400 displayed itself in gleaming red, complete with "No. 2 – Cloverdale" (Victoria's Cloverdale) destination sign, a veritable invitation to hop on and once again make the journey past the Empress Hotel and the Parliament Buildings west to Outer Wharf where the romance of the wide world called and sailing vessels waited, uneasily resisting the Pacific's winds.

Notes

1 The Victoria Daily *Times*, May 16, 1889, p. 4.

2 Victoria *Standard*, May 21, 1889, p. 3.

3 The Victoria *Daily Colonist*, November 22, 1888, p. 4.

4 The Victoria *Daily Colonist*, September 26, 1889, p. 4.

5 The Victoria *Daily Colonist*, October 10, 1890, p. 5.

6 Douglas V. Parker, *No Horsecars in Paradise*, Toronto, 1981, p. 42.

7 *Ibid.*, p. 42.

8 *Ibid.*, p. 44.

9 *Ibid.*, p. 44.

10 *Ibid.*, p. 44.

11 The Victoria *Daily Colonist*, August 7, 1892, p. 1.

12 Parker, *op. cit.*, p. 51.

13 Derek Pethick, *Summer of Promise*, Victoria, 1980, p. 129.

14 Michael Kluckner, *Victoria the Way It Was*, North Vancouver, 1986, p. 136.

15 George Hearn and David Wilkie, *The Cordwood Limited*, Victoria, 1966, p. 16.

16 Kluckner, *op. cit.*, p. 136.

17 Harry Gregson, *A History of Victoria*, Victoria, 1970, p. 135.

18 Parker, *op. cit.*, p. 115.

19 Pemberton's, *The First Sixty Years*, Vancouver, 1947, p. 6.

20 Gregson, *op. cit.*, p. 153.

21 D. F. MacLachlan, *The Esquimalt & Nanaimo Railway: The Dunsmuir Years, 1884-1905*, Victoria, 1986, p. 99.

22 Kluckner, *op. cit.*, p. 83.

23 Hearn and Wilkie, *op. cit.*, p. 31.

24 The Victoria *Daily Colonist*, May 13, 1908, p. 5.

25 The Victoria Daily *Times*, August 18, 1908, p. 2.

26 The Victoria *Daily Colonist*, November 4, 1908, p. 5.

27 The Victoria *Daily Colonist*, March 21, 1909, p. 6.

28 The Victoria *Daily Colonist*, June 6, 1909, p. 3.

29 The Victoria Daily *Times*, May 25, 1909, p. 1.

30 The Victoria *Daily Colonist*, July 11, 1909, p. 3.

31 Hearn and Wilkie, *op. cit.*, p. 51.

32 The Victoria *Daily Colonist*, August 13, 1912, p. 3.

33 The Victoria Daily *Times*, May 3, 1913, p. 7.

34 The Victoria *Daily Colonist*, May 5, 1913, p. 7.

35 The Victoria Daily *Times*, June 14, 1913, p. 8.

36 The Victoria *Daily Colonist*, April 2, 1914, p. 6.

37 The Victoria *Daily Colonist*, January 9, 1915, p. 7.

38 The Victoria *Daily Colonist*, December 31, 1915, p. 3.

39 The Victoria *Daily Colonist*, November 1, 1916, p. 10.

40 Hearn and Wilkie, *op. cit.*, p. 71.

41 The Victoria *Daily Colonist*, January 12, 1924, p. 1.

42 Denny Boyd, *History of Hockey in B.C.*, 1970, p. 17.

43 Cecil Maiden, *Lighted Journey*, Vancouver, 1948, p. 113.

44 Tom MacDonnell, *Daylight Upon Magic*, Toronto, 1989, pp. 150-158.

45 The Victoria Daily *Times*, January 29, 1943, p. 14.

46 The Victoria Daily *Times*, May 20, 1944, p. 6.

47 Robert E. Swanson, letter to J. M. Stewart, October 17, 1946.

48 *The Buzzer*, July 1, 1947.

49 The Victoria Daily *Times*, November 26, 1947, p. 6.

50 The Victoria *Daily Colonist*, May 31, 1959, p. 12.

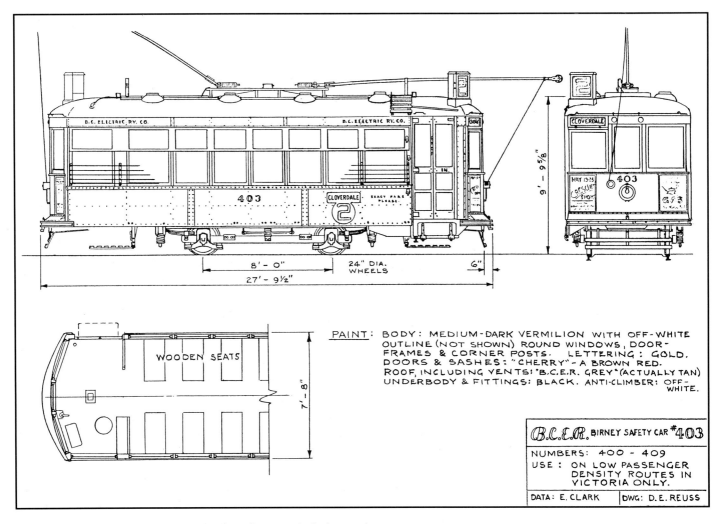

PAINT: BODY: MEDIUM-DARK VERMILION WITH OFF-WHITE
OUTLINE (NOT SHOWN) ROUND WINDOWS, DOOR-
FRAMES & CORNER POSTS. LETTERING: GOLD.
DOORS & SASHES: "CHERRY" - A BROWN RED.
ROOF, INCLUDING VENTS: "B.C.E.R. GREY" (ACTUALLY TAN)
UNDERBODY & FITTINGS: BLACK. ANTI-CLIMBER: OFF-
WHITE.

B.C.E.R. BIRNEY SAFETY CAR #403

NUMBERS: 400 - 409
USE: ON LOW PASSENGER
DENSITY ROUTES IN
VICTORIA ONLY.

DATA: E. CLARK   DWG: D.E. REUSS

Victoria's ten Birney streetcars may not have been particularly popular,
but they certainly were practical – and roughriding.

Roster of Railway Rolling Stock

The roster is based entirely upon B.C. Electric's own equipment records. Where a lack of information exists, "N/A" (not available) appears in the roster. Much credit for its accuracy must be given to retired B.C. Electric employee Ernie Plant, who, half a century ago, began collecting and preserving statistical data of the company's rolling stock.

All the early streetcars were two-man, double-ended vehicles. At the cessation of streetcar service in 1948 in Victoria, all the cars in operation – with the exception of single-ended 188, 200, 201, 250 and 252 - 259 – were still double-ended, albeit one-man operated.

The roster describes cars 1239 - 1244, 1501, 1706 and 1707 as they were on the Saanich line. All other vehicles are presented in their final configuration, in regard to length, weight, type of motors and seating.

Rebuilding of streetcars commenced virtually with the inception of service in 1890. The earliest streetcars first had their open platforms enclosed, creating vestibules, then had their bodies lengthened and more permanent vestibules attached. In addition, small motors were often replaced twice over with more powerful motors. For example, car number 2 arrived with ten-horsepower Thomson-Houston motors, graduated within two years to twenty-horsepower Edison No. 14 motors, and finished her career with thirty-five-horsepower General Electric 1000 motors.

Cars numbered 1 - 11, 14, 15, 17 - 20 and 24 - 50 were single trucked; the rest of the passenger fleet was double-trucked, with the exception of six-wheeled car 16.

With the advent of double-trucked equipment came the classification of streetcar types, in the following fashion:

22, 23	– coach type
69, 70, 71, 73, 75, 107	– Narragansett type
180s, 190s, 230s	– semi-convertible (box) type
250 - 259	– steel frame type
381 - 390	– Brill-Preston type
400 - 409	– all steel Birney type

The only steel-bodied vehicles were Birneys 400 - 409, locomotive 981, S.102, and 0286. Three types of roof design characterized Victoria's equipment, arch (70, 71, 73, 107, 186, 188, 238 and 259 – after rebuilding in the late '30s and early '40s – and 381 - 390, 400 - 409, 1239 - 1244, 1706, 1707, and the roofed work equipment); deck (1 - 20, 24 - 50, 69, 75, 117 - 122, 125, 126, 128, 183 - 185, 187, 189, 191 - 194, 200, 201, 231 - 237, 239, 240 and 250 - 258); and monitor (21 - 23 and 1501). Observation car 123 was roofless.

The types of seats are designated by letter in the roster, L for leather, R for rattan, and W for wooden. Government regulations allowed for 18 standees on cars 22, 23, and 400 - 409; 27 on 188, 189, 231 - 240 and 381 - 390; and 28 on 250 and 252 - 259.

Each of the single-trucked streetcars had two motors, while each of the double-trucked streetcars and interurban coaches had four – with three exceptions: cars 10 and 11 had only one motor each, and car 16 had two.

Of the locomotives and motorized work equipment, all had four motors, with the exception of S.52, S.58, S.59, and the unnumbered construction car, which had two. Snow sweepers S.58 and S.59 each had a third G.E. 57 motor for powering the snow brush.

The following illustrates the types of motors used on the Victoria system, with the horsepower rating of each type. (G.E. = General Electric; WH = Westinghouse)

Edison No. 12	–	20	WH 3	–	25
Edison No. 14	–	20	WH 49	–	35
G.E. 57	–	50	WH 101 B2	–	40
G.E. 67	–	38	WH 101 D2	–	50
G.E. 204 A	–	75	WH 112 B2	–	75
G.E. 800	–	30	WH 301 D2	–	200
G.E. 1000	–	35	WH 508 A	–	25

Streetcars and Interurban Coaches

No.	Builder & Year	Length	Wt. (lbs.)	Motors	Seating	Remarks
1	Patterson & Corbin, 1890	30'	N/A	Edison No. 14	28W	Initially 16' in length, excluding platforms. Out of service, 1916.
2	Patterson & Corbin, 1890	30'	N/A	G.E. 1000	28W	Initially 16' in length, excluding platforms. Out of service, 1916.
3	Patterson & Corbin, 1890	30'	N/A	WH 3	28W	The first streetcar to operate. Initially 16' in length, excluding platforms. Out of service, 1916.
4	Patterson & Corbin, 1890	30'	N/A	G.E. 1000	28W	Initially 16' in length, excluding platforms. Out of service, 1916.
5	St. Louis, 1890	30'	N/A	G.E. 1000	28W	Initially 16' in length, excluding platforms. Out of service, 1916.
6	St. Louis, 1890	30'	N/A	G.E. 1000	28W	Initially 16' in length, excluding platforms. Out of service, 1916.
7	Patterson & Corbin, 1890	32'	N/A	G.E. 1000	32W	Initially 16' in length, excluding platforms. Out of service, 1916.
8	Patterson & Corbin, 1890	30'	N/A	G.E. 1000	28W	Initially 16' in length, excluding platforms. Out of service, 1916.
9	Patterson & Corbin, 1890	30'	N/A	G.E. 1000	28W	Initially 16' in length, excluding platforms. Out of service, 1916.
10	St. Louis, 1891	20'*	N/A	Edison No. 14	35W	Initially unmotored. An open car. Out of service by 1912.
11	St. Louis, 1891	20'*	N/A	Edison No. 14	35W	Initially unmotored. An open car. Out of service, 1916.
12	Brill, 1891	34'	N/A	WH 49	32W	Out of service, 1916.
13	Brill, 1891	34'	N/A	WH 49	32W	Out of service, 1916.
14	St. Louis, 1891	16'*	N/A	G.E. 1000	22W	Out of service by 1912.
15	St. Louis, 1891	16'*	N/A	G.E. 1000	22W	Out of service by 1912.
16	Newburyport, 1892	27'*	N/A	WH 49	N/A	Wrecked in Pt. Ellice Bridge disaster, May 26, 1896.

No.	Builder & Year	Length	Wt. (lbs.)	Motors	Seating	Remarks
17	Pullman, 1891	16'*	N/A	G.E. 1000	22W	Acquired in 1894. Initially operated in Port Townsend, WA. Out of service by 1912.
18	Pullman, 1891	16'*	N/A	G.E. 1000	22W	Acquired in 1894. Initially operated in Port Townsend, WA. Out of service by 1912.
19	Pullman, 1891	16'*	N/A	G.E. 67	22W	Acquired in 1894. Initially operated in Port Townsend, WA. Scrapped in Victoria, October 6, 1913.
20	Canadian General Electric, 1896	21'6"*	N/A	G.E. 800	N/A	Initially an open car, later enclosed. Scrapped in Victoria, May 20, 1912.
21	Ottawa, 1901	29'6"*	N/A	WH 49	44W	Operated only a few days in Victoria before being sent to Vancouver. Number 21 removed and car named "Gladstone." Destroyed in a wreck, November 7, 1908.
22	Ottawa, 1901	40'10"	46,000	WH 101 B2	43R	In service during Victoria's final years of operation. Disposed of in Victoria.
23	Ottawa, 1901	40'10"	46,000	WH 101 B2	43R	In service during Victoria's final years of operation. Disposed of in Victoria.
24	B.C. Electric, 1903	32'	N/A	WH 49	32W	Scrapped in Victoria, February 5, 1913.
25	B.C. Electric, 1903	32'	N/A	G.E. 1000	32W	Scrapped in Victoria, July 25, 1912.
26	B.C. Electric, 1903	32'	N/A	G.E. 1000	32W	Scrapped in Victoria, April 1, 1913.
27	B.C. Electric, 1905	30'	N/A	G.E. 1000	28W	Scrapped in Victoria, October 1915.
28	B.C. Electric, 1905	30'	N/A	G.E. 1000	28W	Out of service by 1912.
29	B.C. Electric, 1905	30'	N/A	G.E. 1000	28W	Scrapped in Victoria, October 1915.
30	B.C. Electric, 1905	30'	N/A	G.E. 1000	28W	Scrapped in Victoria, October 1915.
31	B.C. Electric, 1905	30'	N/A	G.E. 1000	28W	Out of service by 1912.
32	B.C. Electric, 1905	30'	N/A	G.E. 1000	28W	Out of service by 1912.
33	B.C. Electric, 1906	30'	N/A	G.E. 1000	28W	Out of service by 1912.
34	B.C. Electric, 1906	30'	N/A	G.E. 1000	28W	Out of service by 1912.
35	B.C. Electric, 1907	30'	N/A	G.E. 1000	28W	Out of service by 1912.
36	B.C. Electric, 1907	30'	N/A	G.E. 1000	28W	Out of service by 1912.
50	B.C. Electric, 1909	32'	N/A	G.E. 67	32W	Scrapped in Victoria, April 18, 1912.
69	B.C. Electric, 1905	43'4"	46,220	WH 101 B2	38W	Returned to Vancouver in 1921; scrapped October 13, 1948.
70	B.C. Electric, 1906	42'2"	45,000	WH 101 B2	42L	Returned to Vancouver in 1921, rebuilt there in 1940, and scrapped October 2, 1951.
71	B.C. Electric, 1906	42'2"	45,360	WH 101 B2	42L	Returned to Vancouver in 1914, rebuilt there in 1940, and scrapped February 18, 1951.
73	B.C. Electric, 1907	42'2"	44,020	G.E. 67	42L	Returned to Vancouver in 1914, rebuilt there in 1941, and scrapped March 12, 1952.

No.	Builder & Year	Length	Wt. (lbs.)	Motors	Seating	Remarks
75	B.C. Electric, 1905	43'4"	43,450	G.E. 67	41W	Returned to Vancouver in 1912; scrapped March 7, 1949.
107	B.C. Electric, 1908	43'4"	44,920	G.E. 67	42L	Returned to Vancouver in 1921, rebuilt there in 1941, and scrapped September 12, 1951.
117	B.C. Electric, 1909	43'4"	43,450	G.E. 67	42R	Returned to Vancouver, August 8, 1913; scrapped June 20, 1950.
118	B.C. Electric, 1909	43'4"	43,450	G.E. 67	42R	Returned to Vancouver, August 8, 1913; scrapped July 5, 1949.
119	B.C. Electric, 1909	43'4"	43,450	G.E. 67	42R	Returned to Vancouver, August 30, 1913; scrapped February 20, 1950.
120	B.C. Electric, 1909	43'4"	43,450	G.E. 67	42R	Returned to Vancouver, August 28, 1915; scrapped June 6, 1949.
121	B.C. Electric, 1909	43'4"	43,450	G.E. 67	42R	Returned to Vancouver, August 13, 1913; scrapped June 14, 1949.
122	B.C. Electric, 1909	43'4"	43,450	G.E. 67	42R	Returned to Vancouver, August 13, 1913; scrapped July 25, 1949.
123	B.C. Electric, 1909	43'8"	36,500	WH 101 D2	52W	Open observation car. Returned to Vancouver, April 14, 1919; scrapped February 26, 1951.
125	B.C. Electric, 1909	43'4"	43,600	G.E. 67	41W	Returned to Vancouver, January 1931; scrapped December 5, 1949.
126	B.C. Electric, 1909	43'4"	43,600	G.E. 67	41W	Returned to Vancouver, January 1931; scrapped November 24, 1949.
128	B.C. Electric, 1909	43'4"	43,600	G.E. 67	41W	Returned to Vancouver, March 1931; scrapped May 17, 1950.
183	B.C. Electric, 1910	44'6"	46,600	WH 101 B2	38R	Returned to Vancouver in 1921; scrapped October 16, 1948.
184	B.C. Electric, 1910	44'6"	49,820	WH 101 B2	38R	Returned to Vancouver in 1914; scrapped June 13, 1949.
185	B.C. Electric, 1911	44'6"	46,600	WH 101 B2	38R	Returned to Vancouver in 1914; scrapped March 16, 1949.
186	B.C. Electric, 1911	44'6"	46,300	WH 101 B2	40L	Returned to Vancouver in 1914, rebuilt there in 1938, and scrapped September 29, 1950.
187	B.C. Electric, 1910	44'6"	45,500	G.E. 67	38R	Returned to Vancouver in 1914; scrapped October 4, 1948.
188	B.C. Electric, 1910	45'8"	48,850	WH 101 B2	53L	Rebuilt in Vancouver, November 1944. In service during Victoria's final years of operation. Disposed of in Victoria.
189	B.C. Electric, 1910	44'6"	46,600	WH 101 B2	44R	In service during Victoria's final years of operation. Disposed of in Victoria.

No.	Builder & Year	Length	Wt. (lbs.)	Motors	Seating	Remarks
191	B.C. Electric, 1910	44′6″	46,600	WH 101 B2	38R	Returned to Vancouver in 1914; scrapped March 17, 1949.
192	B.C. Electric, 1910	44′6″	47,000	WH 101 B2	38R	Returned to Vancouver, March 1931; scrapped October 1, 1948.
193	B.C. Electric, 1910	44′6″	46,600	WH 101 B2	38R	Returned to Vancouver in 1914; scrapped October 8, 1948.
194	B.C. Electric, 1910	44′6″	47,000	WH 101 B2	38R	Returned to Vancouver, January 1931; scrapped March 4, 1949.
200	Brill, 1911	40′6″	47,500	WH 101 B2	45L	Rebuilt in Vancouver, 1929 and March 1944; sent to Victoria, May 1944. In service during Victoria's final years of operation. Disposed of in Victoria.
201	Brill, 1911	43′	49,540	WH 101 B2	49L	Rebuilt in Vancouver, 1929 and March 1944; sent to Victoria, May 1944. In service during Victoria's final years of operation. Disposed of in Victoria.
231	B.C. Electric, 1911	44′	46,000	WH 101 B2	38R	In service during Victoria's final years of operation. Disposed of in Victoria.
232	B.C. Electric, 1911	44′	46,000	WH 101 B2	38W	In service during Victoria's final years of operation. Disposed of in Victoria.
233	B.C. Electric, 1911	44′	46,000	WH 101 B2	38R	In service during Victoria's final years of operation. Disposed of in Victoria.
234	B.C. Electric, 1911	44′	46,000	WH 101 B2	38R	In service during Victoria's final years of operation. Disposed of in Victoria.
235	B.C. Electric, 1911	44′	46,000	WH 101 B2	38R	In service during Victoria's final years of operation. Disposed of in Victoria.
236	B.C. Electric, 1911	44′	46,000	WH 101 B2	38R	In service during Victoria's final years of operation. Disposed of in Victoria.
237	B.C. Electric, 1911	44′	46,000	WH 101 B2	38R	In service during Victoria's final years of operation. Disposed of in Victoria.
238	B.C. Electric, 1911	47′	48,550	WH 101 B2	48W	Rebuilt in Vancouver, June 1945. In service during Victoria's final years of operation. Disposed of in Victoria.
239	B.C. Electric, 1911	44′	46,000	WH 101 B2	38R	In service during Victoria's final years of operation. Disposed of in Victoria.
240	B.C. Electric, 1911	44′	46,000	WH 101 B2	38R	In service during Victoria's final years of operation. Disposed of in Victoria.
250	B.C. Electric, 1912	44′	48,000	WH 101 B2	48R	In service during Victoria's final years of operation. Disposed of in Victoria.
251	B.C. Electric, 1912	44′6″	48,500	G.E. 67	42R	Returned to Vancouver, March 1931; scrapped September 20, 1950.

No.	Builder & Year	Length	Wt. (lbs.)	Motors	Seating	Remarks
252	B.C. Electric, 1912	44′	48,000	WH 101 B2	48R	In service during Victoria's final years of operation. Disposed of in Victoria.
253	B.C. Electric, 1912	44′	48,000	WH 101 B2	48R	In service during Victoria's final years of operation. Disposed of in Victoria.
254	B.C. Electric, 1912	44′	48,000	WH 101 B2	48R	In service during Victoria's final years of operation. Disposed of in Victoria.
255	B.C. Electric, 1912	44′	48,000	WH 101 B2	48R	In service during Victoria's final years of operation. Disposed of in Victoria.
256	B.C. Electric, 1912	44′	48,000	WH 101 B2	48R	In service during Victoria's final years of operation. Disposed of in Victoria.
257	B.C. Electric, 1912	44′	48,000	WH 101 B2	48R	In service during Victoria's final years of operation. Disposed of in Victoria.
258	B.C. Electric, 1912	44′	48,000	WH 101 B2	48R	In service during Victoria's final years of operation. Disposed of in Victoria.
259	B.C. Electric, 1912	46′	48,000	WH 101 B2	48R	Rebuilt in Vancouver, July 1944. In service during Victoria's final years of operation. Disposed of in Victoria.
381	Preston, 1914	44′2″	48,000	WH 101 B2	48W	Rebuilt in Vancouver, September 1944. In service during Victoria's final years of operation. Disposed of in Victoria.
382	Preston, 1914	44′2″	50,400	G.E. 67	42L	Returned to Vancouver, August 1937. Rebuilt in Vancouver, August 1937; scrapped May 8, 1952.
383	Preston, 1914	44′2″	48,000	WH 101 B2	48W	Rebuilt in Vancouver, October 1944. Last streetcar to operate on the Victoria system. Disposed of in Victoria.
384	Preston, 1914	44′2″	45,680	WH 101 B2	42L	Returned to Vancouver, June 1938. Rebuilt in Vancouver, June 1938; scrapped June 23, 1953.
385	Preston, 1914	44′2″	45,680	WH 101 B2	42L	Returned to Vancouver, August 1937. Rebuilt in Vancouver, December 1937; scrapped May 30, 1949.
386	Preston, 1914	44′2″	45,680	WH 101 B2	42L	Returned to Vancouver, December 1937. Rebuilt in Vancouver, December 1937; scrapped December 4, 1950.
387	Preston, 1914	44′2″	48,000	WH 101 B2	48W	Rebuilt in Vancouver, August 1944. In service during Victoria's final years of operation. Disposed of in Victoria.
388	Preston, 1914	44′2″	48,000	WH 101 B2	36W	In service during Victoria's final years of operation. Disposed of in Victoria.

No.	Builder & Year	Length	Wt. (lbs.)	Motors	Seating	Remarks
389	Preston, 1914	44'2"	48,000	WH 101 B2	48W	Rebuilt in Vancouver, June 1944. In service during Victoria's final years of operation. Disposed of in Victoria.
390	Preston, 1914	44'2"	48,000	WH 101 B2	36W	In service during Victoria's final years of operation. Disposed of in Victoria.
400	Preston, 1922	28'	16,600	WH 508 A	32W	In service during Victoria's final years of operation. The only surviving Victoria streetcar in Nelson, B.C.
401	Preston, 1922	28'	16,600	WH 508 A	32W	In service during Victoria's final years of operation. Disposed of in Victoria.
402	Preston, 1922	28'	16,600	WH 508 A	32W	In service during Victoria's final years of operation. Disposed of in Victoria.
403	Preston, 1922	28'	16,600	WH 508 A	32W	In service during Victoria's final years of operation. Disposed of in Victoria.
404	Preston, 1922	28'	16,600	WH 508 A	32W	In service during Victoria's final years of operation. Disposed of in Victoria.
405	Preston, 1922	28'	16,600	WH 508 A	32W	In service during Victoria's final years of operation. Disposed of in Victoria.
406	Preston, 1922	28'	16,600	WH 508 A	32W	In service during Victoria's final years of operation. Disposed of in Victoria.
407	Preston, 1922	28'	16,600	WH 508 A	32W	In service during Victoria's final years of operation. Disposed of in Victoria.
408	Preston, 1922	28'	16,600	WH 508 A	32W	In service during Victoria's final years of operation. Disposed of in Victoria.
409	Preston, 1922	28'	16,600	WH 508 A	32W	In service during Victoria's final years of operation. Disposed of in Victoria.
1239	St. Louis, 1913	51'	70,800	G.E. 204 A	Saloon 40R Smoking 18W	Sent to Vancouver, January 31, 1923. Given more powerful WH equipment in Vancouver and renumbered 1313, November 1930; scrapped November 2, 1954.
1240	St. Louis, 1913	51'	70,800	G.E. 204 A	Saloon 40R Smoking 18W	Sent to Vancouver, June 6, 1923. Given more powerful WH equipment in Vancouver and renumbered 1314, September 1929; scrapped October 14, 1954.
1241	St. Louis, 1913	51'	70,800	G.E. 204 A	Saloon 40R Smoking 18W	Sent to Vancouver, June 18, 1923. Given more powerful WH equipment in Vancouver and renumbered 1315, August 1929; scrapped February 1955.

No.	Builder & Year	Length	Wt. (lbs.)	Motors	Seating	Remarks
1242	St. Louis, 1913	51'	70,800	G.E. 204 A	Saloon 40R Smoking 18W	Sent to Vancouver, June 30, 1923. Given more powerful WH equipment in Vancouver and renumbered 1316, August 1929; scrapped February 1955.
1243	St. Louis, 1913	51'	70,800	G.E. 204 A	Saloon 40R Smoking 18W	Sent to Vancouver, June 18, 1923. Given more powerful WH equipment in Vancouver and renumbered 1317, 1929; scrapped February 1955.
1244	St. Louis, 1913	51'	70,800	G.E. 204 A	Saloon 40R Smoking 18W	Sent to Vancouver, June 18, 1923. Given more powerful WH equipment in Vancouver and renumbered 1318, December 1929; scrapped September 18, 1954.
1501	B.C. Electric, 1907	50'4"	70,000	G.E. 204 A	30R	Built as passenger coach, "Sumas"; numbered 1216, 1910; rebuilt and renumbered 1501, 1913, as a mail-passenger coach; rebuilt and renumbered 1216, 1928. Scrapped in Vancouver, September 1958. Car 1501 arrived in Victoria, October 4, 1914, and arrived back in Vancouver, April 25, 1928.
1706	Niles, 1912	54'3"	83,700	G.E. 204 A	Baggage & Express Only	Sent to Vancouver, June 1923. Given more powerful WH equipment in Vancouver, 1923; scrapped in Vancouver, January 30, 1952.
1707	Niles, 1912	54'3"	83,700	G.E. 204 A	Baggage & Express Only	Given more powerful WH equipment in Vancouver, November 1913; scrapped in New Westminster, August 1956. Car 1707 had been shipped to Victoria from Vancouver on June 30, 1913 and was back in Vancouver on September 27, 1913.

* Length of car body only, excluding platforms.

Locomotives and Work Cars

No.	Builder & Year	Length	Wt. (lbs.)	Motors	Remarks
905	B.C. Electric, 1909	28'10"	40,500	WH 101 B2	Locomotive. In service during Victoria's final years of operation. Disposed of in Victoria. Used latterly as wrecking car.
906	B.C. Electric, 1909	37'10"	50,000	WH 101 B2	Locomotive. Completely rebuilt, July 25, 1912, and sent to Victoria. In storage in Victoria during final years of operation; had been used latterly as a tower car. Disposed of in Victoria.
953	B.C. Electric, 1911	29'3"	79,140	WH 112 B2	Locomotive. Shipped to Victoria, April 20, 1913, for Saanich line use. Disposed of in Victoria.
981	Baldwin, 1911	31'1"	96,340	WH 301 D2	Locomotive. Shipped to Victoria, April 20, 1913, for Saanich line use. Returned to New Westminster, July 29, 1919. Scrapped in Vancouver, 1950s.
L.5	B.C. Electric, 1912	42'	68,500	G.E. 57	Line car. In service during Victoria's final years of operation. Disposed of in Victoria. Originally numbered 532.
S.52	B.C. Electric, 1907	20'5"	28,000	G.E. 57	Sprinkler car; then, weed sprayer on Saanich line, and, later, rail grinder. In storage in Victoria during final years of operation. Disposed of in Victoria. Originally numbered 102.
S.58	Ottawa, 1913	28'1"	35,320	G.E. 57	Snow sweeper. In service during Victoria's final years of operation. Disposed of in Victoria.
S.59	B.C. Electric, 1923	28'1"	35,320	G.E. 57	Snow sweeper. Castings from Ottawa Car Co.; body built at New Westminster. Vehicle assembled and electrical equipment installed in Victoria. In service during Victoria's final years of operation. Disposed of in Victoria.
S.60	B.C. Electric, 1905	26'	20,500	G.E. 67	Motorized flat car. Scrapped in Victoria in the 1920s.
S.61	B.C. Electric, 1899	35'8"	36,000	G.E. 67	Wrecking car; also known as motorized freight car and auxiliary service car. Motors removed in early 1940s: car not serviceable during Victoria's final years of operation. Disposed of in Victoria. Originally 3, then 101.
S.102	C.C.&F., 1912	35'6"	26,000	WH 112 B2	Dump car. Scrapped in Victoria in the 1920s. (C.C.&F. = Canadian Car & Foundry.)

No.	Builder & Year	Length	Wt. (lbs.)	Motors	Remarks
0286	Simplex, N/A	N/A	N/A	No motors	Steel dump car. Used occasionally to haul sand. On site during Victoria's final years of operation. Disposed of in Victoria. Replaced S.102.
6111	Hicks, N/A	N/A	N/A	No motors	Maintenance-of-way flat car, but rarely used. On site during Victoria's last years of operation. Disposed of in Victoria. Replaced S.60.
No #	B.C. Electric, 1900	25'	N/A	Edison No.12	Construction car. Final disposition unknown. In service at the turn of the century.
No #	N/A, 1900	N/A	N/A	No motors	Centre dump car. Final disposition unknown. In service at the turn of the century.
No #	N/A, 1900	N/A	N/A	No motors	Centre dump car. Final disposition unknown. In service at the turn of the century.
No #	N/A, N/A	N/A	N/A	No motors	Side dump car. Final disposition unknown. In service at the turn of the century.
No #	N/A, N/A	N/A	N/A	No motors	Side dump car. Final disposition unknown. In service at the turn of the century.
No #	N/A, N/A	N/A	N/A	No motors	Flat car. Final disposition unknown. In service at the turn of the century.
No #	N/A, N/A	N/A	N/A	No motors	Snow broom. Final disposition unknown. In service at the turn of the century.

Bibliography

ARTICLES

British Columbia Electric Railway Company Limited Papers (B.C. Provincial Archives, Victoria, and the Library of the University of British Columbia, Vancouver, Special Collections Division).

Binns, R. M. "The Point Ellice Bridge Disaster." *Canadian Rail*, April 1969, pp. 98-107.

Brown, Spike. "When the British Columbia Electric Was Young." *The Dispatcher*, July-August 1964, pp. 14-21.

Green, George. "Some Pioneers of Light and Power." *British Columbia Historical Quarterly*. July 1938, pp. 145-62.

Henson, Fred C. "Tote 'em Railroad." *The Railway Conductor*, April 1950, pp. 104-08.

Hoffmeister, John E. "The Far-West Trolley." *Canadian Rail*, September 1973, pp. 277-84.

———. "Car 400 Comes Home!" *Canadian Rail*, February 1974, pp. 53-56.

Johnson, Norman K. "B.C. Electric Today." *ERA Headlights*, November 1954, pp. 1-2.

Neuberger, Richard L. "British Columbia Electric Rolls On." *Railroad Magazine*, March 1948, pp. 90-98.

Pugsley, Edmund E. "Electric Lines of British Columbia." *Railroad Magazine*, October 1946, pp. 99-106.

Roy, Patricia E. "Direct Management from Abroad: The Formative Years of the British Columbia Electric Railway." *The Business History Review*, Summer 1973, pp. 239-59.

Sharman, Vic. "B.C.E.R. Notes." *Interurbans*, May 1947, p. 55.

Wright, Monte J. *The Birney Car, 1921-1948*. Victoria, B.C.: British Columbia Provincial Museum, 1974.

———. *Street Railways in Victoria, 1888-1948*. Victoria, B.C.: British Columbia Provincial Museum, n.d.

BOOKS

Barrett, Anthony A. and Liscombe, R. W. *Francis Rattenbury and British Columbia: Artchitecture and Challenge in the Imperial Age*. Vancouver, B.C.: University of British Columbia Press, 1983.

Bell, Betty. *The Fair Land, Saanich*. Victoria, B.C.: Sono Nis Press, 1982.

Boyd, Denny. *History of Hockey in B.C.* Vancouver, B.C.: Canucks Publishing Ltd., 1970.

Carstens, Harold H., ed. *Traction Planbook*. 2nd ed. Fredon, N.J.: Carstens Publications, Inc., 1975.

Castle, Geoffrey, ed. *Saanich: An Illustrated History*. Sidney, B.C.: Manning Press Limited, 1989.

Cavin, Ruth. *Trolleys*. New York, N.Y.: Hawthorn Books, Inc., 1976.

City and Interurban Cars. San Marino, California: Pacific Railway Journal, 1961.

Connelly, Dolly. *Guidebook to Vancouver Island*. Los Angeles, California: Ward Ritchie Press, 1973.

Cotton, Peter. *Vice Regal Mansions of British Columbia*. Vancouver, B.C.: Elgin Publications Limited, 1981.

Cross, W. K., Goulson, C. F. and Loft, A. E., eds. *The British Columbia Source Book*. Victoria, B.C.: Printer to the Queen's Most Excellent Majesty, 1966.

Davies, David L. *Historical Summary—Railways in British Columbia*. Vancouver, B.C.: Canadian Railroad Historical Association, Pacific Coast Branch, 1973.

Dorman, Robert. *A Statutory History of the Steam and Electric Railways of Canada 1836-1937*. Ottawa, Ontario: Canada Department of Transport, 1938.

Due, John F. *The Intercity Electric Railway Industry in Canada*. Toronto, Ontario: University of Toronto Press, 1966.

Effle, Mark, ed. *I.N.L.: The Early Interurban Newsletters 1943-1944*. Glendale, California: Interurbans Publications, 1978.

Ewert, Henry. *The Story of the B.C. Electric Railway Company*. North Vancouver, B.C.: Whitecap Books Limited, 1986.

Forward, C. N., ed. *Residential and Neighbourhood Studies in Victoria*. Victoria, B.C.: University of Victoria, 1973.

Gosnell, R. E. *The Year Book of British Columbia*. Victoria, B.C.: British Columbia Legislative Assembly, 1911.

Gregson, Harry. *A Hisotry of Victoria, 1842-1970*. Vancouver, B.C.: J. J. Douglas Ltd., 1970.

Gross, Joseph. *Trolley and Interurban Lines of the United States and Canada*, rev. ed. Spencerport, N.Y.: Joseph Gross, 1977.

Hacking, Norman R. and Lamb, W. Kaye. *The Princess Story*. Vancouver, B.C.: Mitchell Press Limited, 1974.

Harvey, R. D. *A History of Saanich Peninsula Railways*. Victoria, B.C.: Department of Commercial Transport, Railways Branch, 1960.

Hearn, George and Wilkie, David. *The Cordwood Limited*. Victoria, B.C.: British Columbia Railway Historical Association, 1966.

Holloway, Godfrey. *The Empress of Victoria*. Victoria, B.C.: Pacifica Productions Limited, 1968.

Horth, Nell. *North Saanich*. Sidney, B.C.: Porthole Press Limited, 1988.

Jackman, S. W. *Vancouver Island*. Harrisburg, Pennsylvania: Stackpole Books, 1972.

Johnson, Patricia M. *Canada's Pacific Province*. Toronto, Ontario: McClelland and Stewart Limited, 1966.

Jordan, W. *Statistics for the B.C. Railway Historian*. Vancouver, B.C.: Canadian Railroad Historical Association, Pacific Coast Branch, 1973.

Kluckner, Michael. *Victoria: The Way It Was*. North Vancouver, B.C.: Whitecap Books Limited, 1986.

Lai, Chuen-yan David. *Arches in British Columbia*. Victoria, B.C.: Sono Nis Press, 1982.

Lillard, Charles. *Seven Shillings a Year*. Ganges, B.C.: Horsdal & Schubart Publishers Limited, 1986.

Lind, Alan R. *From Horsecars to Streamliners: An Illustrated History of the St. Louis Car Company*. Park Forest, Illinois: Transport History Press, 1978.

MacDonnell, Tom. *Daylight Upon Magic*. Toronto, Ontario: Macmillan, 1989.

MacLachlan, D. F. *The Esquimalt & Nanaimo Railway: The Dunsmuir Years, 1884-1905*. Victoria, B.C.: British Columbia Railway Historical Association, 1986.

McGregor, D. A. *They Gave Royal Assent*. Vancouver, B.C.: Mitchell Press Limited, 1967.

Maiden, Cecil. *Lighted Journey*. Vancouver, B.C.: British Columbia Electric Company Limited, 1948.

Melvin, George E. *The Post Offices of B.C., 1858-1970*. Vernon, B.C.: Wayside Press, 1972.

Middleton, William D. *The Interurban Era*. Milwaukee, Wisconsin: Kalmbach Publishing Co., 1961.

———. *The Time of the Trolley*. Milwaukee, Wisconsin: Kalmbach Publishing Co. 1967.

Miller, John Anderson. *Fares, Please!*. New York, N.Y.: D. Appleton-Century Company, Inc., 1941.

Modern Types of City and Interurban Cars and Trucks, John Stephenson Company. Felton, California: Glenwood Publishers, 1972.

Montgomery, R. H. *Altitudes in Southern British Columbia*. Ottawa, Ontario: Canada Department of Mines and Resources, 1948.

Morgan, Roland and Disher, Emily. *Victoria, Then and Now*. Vancouver, B.C.: Bodima Publications, 1977.

Myers, Thomas R. *Ninety Years of Public Utility Service on Vancouver Island: A History of the B.C. Electric*. Victoria, B.C.: B.C. Electric, 1954.

Parker, D. *Nelson Street Railway*. Victoria, B.C.: British Columbia Railway Historical Association, 1961.

Parker, Douglas V. *No Horsecars in Paradise*. Toronto, Ontario: Railfare Enterprises Limited, 1981.

Pemberton's. *The First Sixty Years* Vancouver, B.C.: 1947.

Pethick, Derek. *British Columbia Disasters*. Langley, B.C.: Mr. Paperback, 1982.

———. *Summer of Promise*. Victoria, B.C.: Sono Nis Press, 1980.

Province of British Columbia. *Manual of Provincial Information, 1930*. Victoria, B.C.: Provincial Bureau of Information, 1930.

Reksten, Terry. *More English Than The English*. Victoria, B.C.: Orca Book Publishers, 1986.

———. *Rattenbury*. Victoria, B.C.: Sono Nis Press, 1978.

Robinson, Lewis J., ed. *British Columbia*. Toronto, Ontario: University of Toronto Press, 1972.

Rowsome, Frank. *Trolley Car Treasury*. New York, N.Y.: Bonanza Books, 1956.

Sanford, Barrie. *The Pictorial History of Railroading in British Columbia*. Vancouver, B.C.: Whitecap Books Ltd., 1981.

Stevens, G. R. *Canadian National Railways, vol. 2*. Toronto, Ontario: Clarke, Irwin and Company Limited, 1962.

Turner, Robert D. *Vancouver Island Railroads*. San Marino, California: Golden West Books, 1973.

———. *The Pacific Princesses*. Victoria, B.C.: Sono Nis Press, 1977.

White, James. *Altitudes in the Dominion of Canada*. Ottawa, Ontario: Commission of Conservation Canada, 1915.

Wilson, Robert S. *Trolley Trails Through the West: Trolleys of Western Canada*. Yakima, Washington: Wilson Brothers Publications, 1979.

NEWSPAPERS AND JOURNALS

Brill's Magazine

B.C. Electric Employees' Magazine (also B.C. Electric Employees Magazine, and B.C.E. Family Post)

British Columbia Historical Quarterly

The British Columbia Mining and Engineering Record

B.C. Studies

The Business History Review

The Buzzer

The Camosun

Canadian Electrical News

Canadian Rail

Canadian Railway and Marine World

Canadian Transportation

The Coupler

The Dispatcher

Electric Railroads

ERA Headlights

Intercom

Interurbans

Juan de Fuca News–Review

The Mirror (Sooke)

The Mining Record

The News (Victoria)

The Official Guide of the Railways

Pacific News

Progress

Railroad Magazine

Sidney & Islands Review

Traction and Models

Traction Heritage

Trains

Transit Exchange

The Victoria Daily Colonist (also The Daily British Colonist, The Daily Colonist, and The Colonist)

The Victoria Daily Times

The Victoria Standard

The Week

The Western Historical Quarterly

THESIS

Roy, Patricia E. "The British Columbia Electric Railway Company, 1897-1928; A British Company in British Columbia." Unpublished Ph.D. thesis, The University of British Columbia, 1970.

MISCELLANEOUS

Ministry of Railway (files in the collection of B.C. Provincial Archives)

Railway timetables
Canadian National
Canadian Northern
Canadian Pacific
Great Northern

Statistics Canada records

Index